ABOUT CHURCH
HISTORY

FR. DAVID VINCENT MECONI, S.J.

Scripture quotations, unless otherwise noted, are from the Catholic Edition of the Revised Standard Version of the Bible, copyright © 1965, 1966 the Division of Christian Education of the National Council of Churches of Christ in the United States of America. Used by permission. All rights reserved.

Excerpts from the English translation of the *Catechism of the Catholic Church* for use in the United States of America copyright © 1994, United States Catholic Conference, Inc.—Libreria Editrice Vaticana. Used with permission.

Cover and interior design by Caroline Kiser

Cover image: statue of Saint Denis beheaded, patron and first bishop of Paris, in the Crypte of the Sacre Coeur. Photo © Jose Ignacio Soto / Shutterstock. Back cover image: The Colosseum, built 70-80 AD (photo), Roman, (1st century) / Rome, Italy / Bridgeman Images.

ISBN: 978-1-61890-733-2

Published in the United States by
Saint Benedict Press, LLC
PO Box 410487
Charlotte, NC 28241
www.SaintBenedictPress.com

Printed and bound in the United States of America

FOR TULLIO MECONI
POLYMATH, POLYGLOT,
PURVEYOR OF HISTORY,
AND LOVER OF ALL
THINGS BEAUTIFUL

Preface

Within his collection of one hundred short stories, Giovanni Boccaccio (d. 1375) tells the tale of a shrewd Jewish businessman and lifelong Parisian named Abraham. Desirous of entering the Catholic Church, Abraham's business savvy finds it reasonable to visit Rome first to see for himself exactly what kind of people Catholics really are. A devout and dear friend of Abraham's, Giannotto di Civignì, begs him not to go to Rome but to simply present himself to the archbishop of Paris for immediate baptism. Giannotto admits his fear that Abraham will make it to Rome and see the graft and corruption of the pope and the Curia, and would then be too scandalized ever to become Catholic. Disregarding this advice, Abraham travels to the Eternal City and soaks in as much Italian Catholicism as he can stand. He comments not only on the beautiful churches and works of art but also on the prelates who were drunks and gluttons, lax in their prayers and even worse in their morals.

Upon returning to Paris and to the home of Giannotto, Abraham rushes in and declares that he is more eager than ever to be baptized.

Incredulous, Giannotto asks how this can be.

"I see that what these scoundrel clerics so zealously want never takes root. But the exact opposite happens: despite them, your Church grows continually and shines more and more brightly." Therefore, Abraham concludes, "it is quite clear to me that your Church must have the Holy Spirit for its foundation and support," arguing that it would have collapsed centuries ago were it not for this divine foundation (*Decameron*, First Day, Novel Two).

This is a good piece of theology to keep in mind when surveying Church history: it is ultimately God who inaugurates, sustains, guides, and brings His Church to completion. As such, the history of the Church is just as much about the fidelity of God as the antics of God's people. The following collection of facts attest to how the Catholic Church has survived horrible popes and violent dictators, and has been home to billions of sinners in need of a community where they could finally know love.

From the invention of hospitals to hypertexts, from ancient Gospels to the founding of modern genetics, the Catholic Church has made

The Seven Joys of the Virgin, 1480, by Hans Memling (1435/1440-1494), Memling, Hans (c.1433-94) / Alte Pinakothek, Munich, Germany / Photo © Tarker / Bridgeman Images

all our lives more beautiful, meaningful, and efficient. Each of us is surrounded by Catholic events and images, often unaware of how the Faith has formed our culture.

For example, *Christmas* literally means Christ's Mass, Halloween is really All Hallow's Eve, and, where there is a time for feasting, there is also a time for fasting. *Mardi Gras* is of course French for "Fat Tuesday" because we fast the next day—Ash Wednesday—and the term *Carnival* is derived from two Latin words (*caro*, meat, and *vale*, goodbye) because it is the time of year we say goodbye to the tastier things of life until Easter morning. The Spanish *adios* and the French *adieu* both send you off with the blessing of God (*Deus* in Latin), as does even our own "goodbye." Ancient Christianity permeates who we are today, informing how we keep time, celebrate occasions, speak, see the world, and more.

Church history is full of both important achievements as well as many unfortunate atrocities. *101 Surprising Facts About Church History* is meant to show how much the Church of Jesus Christ has done for all of God's children. From basic human rights to the judgment of cultures by how they treat the most vulnerable of people entrusted to them, traditional Christian beliefs have given voice to the inherent dignity of every human person more than any other creed or set of principles. The Church helped end modern forms of slavery, condemned as abhorrent all forms of child sacrifice, and elevated the status of women by condemning polygamy, artificial birth control, and abortion.

Jesus Christ wills the eternal joy and salvation of every human person. He founded a Church for no other reason than to save souls. The Church is the means by which Christ reduplicates His own life in others. It is here in this visible community of saints and sinners that the world comes to witness Christ tirelessly pasturing His people back to Him. As such, enjoy this traipse through two thousand years of Church history, coming to see the beauty and the richness of this eternally important drama.

Fr. David Vincent Meconi, S.J.

St. Ignatius of Loyola
July 31, 2016

1 The first name for Christians was "People of the Way"

Before they were known as Christians, Jesus's followers were called "People of the Way" (cf. Acts 9:2). They first became known as Christians in Antioch (see Acts 11:26) and were later called Catholics. The Greek word *katholikos* means "according to the whole" or "universal," while the word "church" is an anglicized version of the Greek *ekklesia*, which means "to be called out from this world."

(*above*) St. Paul preaching in the synagogue at Antioch, illustration from 'Harold Copping Pictures: The Crown Series', c.1920's (colour litho), Copping, Harold (1863-1932) / Private Collection / Bridgeman Images

(*above*) Saint Pierre Church in Antakya (Hatay) Turkey. This cave, which was used by the very first disciples to be called Christians, is one of Christianity's oldest churches. De Agostini Picture Library / Bridgeman Images

THE CHURCH IS CATHOLIC: SHE PROCLAIMS THE FULLNESS OF THE FAITH. SHE BEARS IN HERSELF AND ADMINISTERS THE TOTALITY OF THE MEANS OF SALVATION. SHE IS SENT OUT TO ALL PEOPLES. SHE SPEAKS TO ALL MEN. SHE ENCOMPASSES ALL TIMES.

—CATECHISM OF THE CATHOLIC CHURCH, 868

The Catholic Church is the oldest institution in the Western world

The Catholic Church is the only *ekklesia* that teaches she is the one, visible, and uninterrupted Church founded by Jesus Christ. The Church is thus the oldest institution in the Western world, tracing her roots back to Christ's founding recorded in Matthew: "And I tell you, you are Peter, and on this rock I will build my Church" (16:18). As the English writer and Catholic convert G.K. Chesterton came to realize, the Catholic Church is the only institution capable of freeing us from the "degrading slavery" of being children of our age, and the only one on earth who talks "as if it were the truth; as if it were a real messenger refusing to tamper with a real message."

(*below*) Giving of the Keys to St. Peter, from the Sistine Chapel, 1481 (fresco), Perugino, Pietro (c.1445-1523) / Vatican Museums and Galleries, Vatican City / Bridgeman Images

3 The Catholic Church has many major rites

Christ's Church is much wider than the Latin or Roman rite with which most westerners are familiar. There are two other ancient Eastern rites originating from the earliest sees of Christianity: the Antiochene and Alexandrian rites. Under the guidance of St. Basil the Great and St. John Chrysostom, an influential bishop of Constantinople, the Byzantine rite arose a bit later, as did the Armenian and Syrian rites further east. The term "rite" refers to the prayers, ceremonies, and practices of a religious body. Such rites (see table, opposite page) are not different Churches but ancient and diverse ways the one Church has always worshiped, so as to respect the traditional customs of a local people.

(*below*) The Fathers of the Church: Saint Basil of Caesarea, Saint John Chrysostom, Saint Gregorius of Nazianzus—an icon of 17th cent. from Lipie, Historic Museum in Sanok, Poland. Public domain via Wikimedia Commons.

Genealogy of the Christian Churches

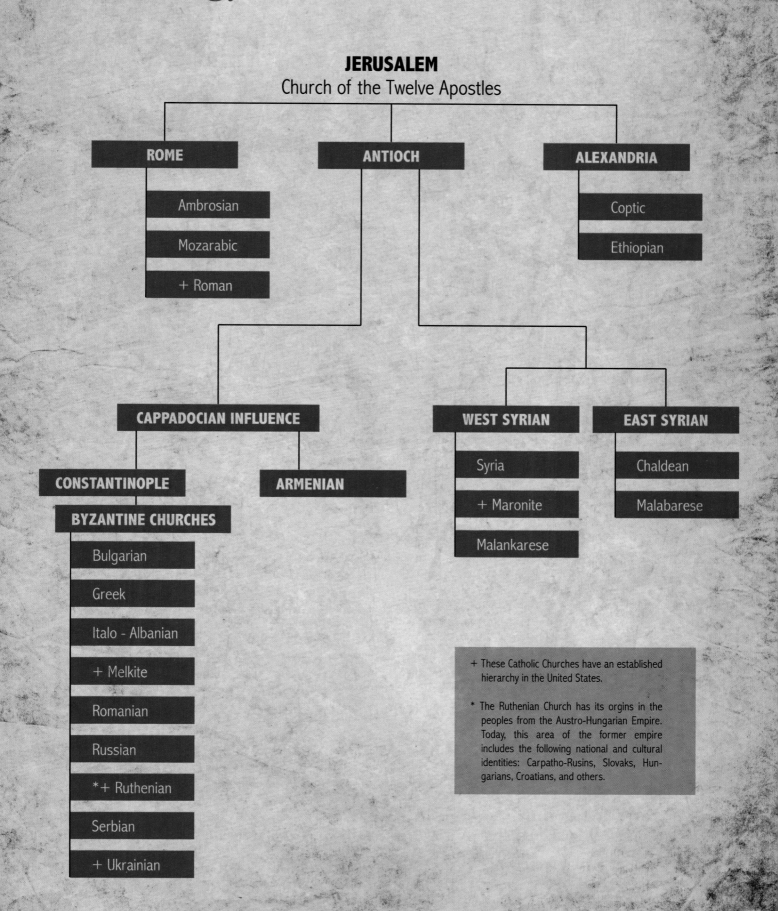

JERUSALEM
Church of the Twelve Apostles

ROME

Ambrosian

Mozarabic

+ Roman

ANTIOCH

ALEXANDRIA

Coptic

Ethiopian

CAPPADOCIAN INFLUENCE

WEST SYRIAN

Syria

+ Maronite

Malankarese

EAST SYRIAN

Chaldean

Malabarese

CONSTANTINOPLE

BYZANTINE CHURCHES

Bulgarian

Greek

Italo - Albanian

+ Melkite

Romanian

Russian

*+ Ruthenian

Serbian

+ Ukrainian

ARMENIAN

+ These Catholic Churches have an established hierarchy in the United States.

* The Ruthenian Church has its orgins in the peoples from the Austro-Hungarian Empire. Today, this area of the former empire includes the following national and cultural identities: Carpatho-Rusins, Slovaks, Hungarians, Croatians, and others.

(*above*) Landscape with Saint John on Patmos, 1640 (oil on canvas), Poussin, Nicolas (1594-1665) / The Art Institute of Chicago, IL, USA / A. A. Munger Collection / Bridgeman Images

4 St. John was the only Apostle who did not die a martyr

Peter and Paul made their way to Rome after A.D. 60 to evangelize at the heart of the empire. In the year 64, a devastating fire broke out in Rome and the emperor Nero, blaming the Christians, used it as an occasion to squelch this new religion. During this persecution, Paul was beheaded since he was a Roman citizen and therefore not liable to crucifixion, and Peter was crucified on Vatican Hill. Feeling unworthy of imitating Jesus in those final moments, Pope Peter asked to be crucified upside down. Legends of the other Apostles tell of their bloody martyrdom, except for St. John, who died in exile on the island of Patmos around the year 100.

St. Peter's is not the pope's cathedral

Every bishop in the Catholic Church has one cathedral. Surprisingly, the pope's cathedral is not St. Peter's Basilica in Vatican City but rather the Archbasilica of St. John in the Lateran, which was donated to the Church in the fourth century by the emperor Constantine. St. Peter's is viewed more as the cathedral of all Christians worldwide.

(*below*) View at the San Giovanni in Laterano Basilica in Rome, Italy. Photo © grafalex / Shutterstock.

6 The Greek word for fish spells out a title for Jesus

The five letters of the Greek word for fish—ΙΧΘΥΣ—spell out a beautiful title for Jesus. In Greek, each letter can be acrostically taken as:

I   Jesus

X   Christ

Θ   *Th* for *Theos*, the Greek word for God

Υ   A capital *U* for *uios*, the Greek word for son

Σ   The Greek letter *S* here stands for *soter*, or savior

This, then, spells out "Jesus Christ, the Son of God, (our) Savior." Other ancient symbols found on the walls of Christian places, sarcophagi, and religious objects were dolphins, whose elegance symbolized the elects' movement from earth to heaven; the mother pelican, whose large beak pricks her chest while feeding her young, symbolizing Christ's feeding His people with His own body and blood; bees, whose honey symbolized the sweetness of the Christian message; and the peacock, who grows more beautiful feathers as the old ones die—a symbol of the Resurrection.

(*below*) Funerary stele bearing one of the earliest Christian inscriptions. Upper tier: dedication to the Dis Manibus and Christian motto in Greek letters C Ω Ω / Ikhthus zōntōn ("fish of the living"); middle tier: depiction of fish and an anchor. Licinia Amias, from the area of the Vatican necropolis, Rome (marble), 3rd century AD / Baths of Diocletian, National Roman Museum, Rome, Italy / Photo © Zev Radovan / Bridgeman Images

(*above*) Triumph of Faith - Christian Martyrs in the Time of Nero, 65 AD (oil on canvas), Thirion, Eugene Romain (1839-1910) / Private Collection / Photo © Bonhams, London, UK / Bridgeman Images

The Romans accused the early Christians of cannibalism

7

Christians were persecuted because they refused to worship the gods and goddesses of the Roman pantheon. Seeing that they were faithful citizens, however, their Roman persecutors needed to increase the severity of their claims. Since the persecutors knew that the Eucharist was at the heart of Christian discipleship, they accused the followers of Jesus of cannibalism because they ate the flesh of Christ (see Jn 6:22–71) and of incest because of the "kiss of peace" given to one's brothers and sisters at Mass, as well as their preference for marrying other Christians (see 2 Cor 6:14–15).

"They then falsely accused us, when the soldiers so urged them of cannibalistic feasts and of incestuous intercourse, and of things of which it is not lawful either to speak or to think."

—EUSEBIUS' HISTORY OF THE CHURCH, BOOK 5.1

8 Christian martyrdom helped spread the Church rather than suppress it

The Greek word for one who witnesses to another is *martyr*. Martyrdom is considered one of the crucial influences in the growth and development of the early Church and Christian beliefs. St. Polycarp of Smyrna was bound and tied to the Romans' funeral pyre, but the flames only encircled his body like the massive sails of a ship, and his flesh took on the aroma of baking bread. In the year 258, the great deacon of Rome St. Lawrence was sentenced to death. As the flames from the gridiron began to engulf Lawrence, he taunted his persecutors by telling them, "Turn me over, I think I am done on this side!" While these persecutions and executions were aimed at suppressing the Faith, sacrificial acts like these spurred mass conversions and gave other persecuted Christians the courage they needed to spread the Church.

(*below*) St. Lawrence on the Grill, 1617 (marble), Bernini, Gian Lorenzo (1598-1680) / Galleria degli Uffizi, Florence, Italy / Bridgeman Images

(*above*) Christ Pantocrator (encaustic on panel), Byzantine School, (6th century) / Monastery of Saint Catherine, Mount Sinai, Egypt / Photo © Zev Radovan / Bridgeman Images. (*left*) Madonna and child icon, Sisters of Nazareth Convent (photo) / Godong/UIG / Bridgeman Images

Icons and other forms of art helped spread the gospel

9

The earliest legend about an image of the face of Christ tells us that the king of Edessa asked Jesus to heal him from a disfiguring disease (probably leprosy). Christ sent an image of His own face imprinted on a piece of cloth, known today as the Mandylion. Since most ancients were illiterate, Christians came to know Scripture through paint-ings and icons. They didn't pray to images and icons, as some people protested, but merely used it as a tangible device to make otherwise unseen realities visibly present to those on earth. In 787, the Second Council of Nicaea helped clarify the use of icons, frescos, and other forms of art in spreading the gospel.

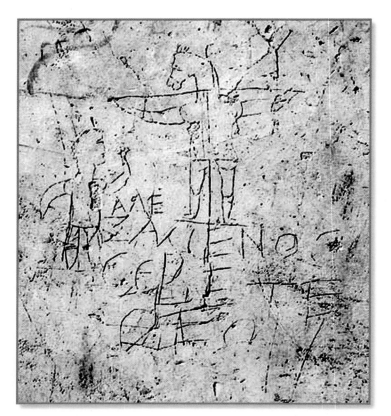

(*above*) The Alexamenos graffito is an inscription carved in plaster on a wall of an ancient Roman school, Palatine Antiquarium. It dates from c. 1st to 2nd C. A.D. The drawing showing a person worshiping a crucified ass is accepted by many scholars as a mocking depiction of Christianity. The translation of the Greek inscription reads, "Alexamenos worships his God." Alexamenos graffiti, Palatine Antiquarium, Rome (litho) / Private Collection / Photo © Zev Radovan / Bridgeman Images.

10 Anti-Christian graffiti is as old as Christianity

The earliest anti-Christian piece of graffiti was found on the Capitoline Hill and dates back to the late first century. In this crude etching, a Christian by the name of Alexamenos is depicted praying pitifully to a crucified donkey with the caption reading, "Alexamenos worships his god." This insult from the Roman mind shows us that Christianity endured mockery of the sacred not long after the time of Christ, just as we do today as well.

Justin was the first Christian apologist

Martyred in Rome for his robust defense of the Christian faith, Justin left three treatises (and various fragments) that still survive to this day. His *First Apology* argues that Jesus is the Word made flesh, the one who has inspired goodness, beauty, and reason in all human persons. The *Second Apology* asserts that Christians are not guilty of the atrocities attributed to them by fearful men who only want to destroy the good. In his *Dialogue with Trypho*, Justin journeys through all of salvation history, showing how Christianity is the consummation of the Jewish Scriptures.

"To yield and give way to our passions is the lowest slavery, even as to rule over them is the only liberty."

— ST. JUSTIN MARTYR, FRAGMENT 18

(*right*) Saint Justin the Martyr. One of statues in the Cathedral of Milan (Italy). © Tupungato / Shutterstock.

12 Irenaeus was the first to call Mary "the New Eve"

Bishop Irenaeus of Lyons was one of the earliest to honor Mary. To help young Christian communities, he compiled a catalog of current heresies in five lengthy books titled *Against the Heresies*. Irenaeus approached the Christian faith by way of "recapitulation," declaring that everything Adam and Eve lost, the New Adam, Jesus, and the New Eve, Mary, restored through their obedience to the Father. Mary's "yes" thus reunites all that our first mother lost for us. In this way, Irenaeus was the first to call Mary "the New Eve."

(*above*) Altarpiece of the Annunciation or the Prado Altarpiece, 1430-1432, by Giovanni da Fiesole known as Fra Angelico (1400-ca 1455) , Angelico, Fra (Guido di Pietro) (c.1387-1455) / Prado, Madrid, Spain / De Agostini Picture Library / Bridgeman Images

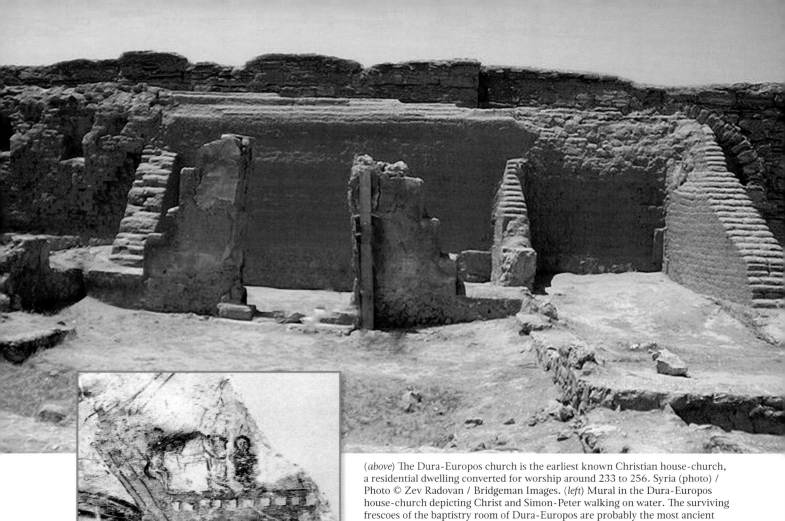

(*above*) The Dura-Europos church is the earliest known Christian house-church, a residential dwelling converted for worship around 233 to 256. Syria (photo) / Photo © Zev Radovan / Bridgeman Images. (*left*) Mural in the Dura-Europos house-church depicting Christ and Simon-Peter walking on water. The surviving frescoes of the baptistry room of Dura-Europos are probably the most ancient Christian paintings. (235 CE) / Pictures from History / Bridgeman Images.

The oldest church structure began in a home

13

The oldest known church structure began as a family home in Dura-Europos, in what is now Syria. Discovered during an archaeological dig in the early twentieth century, the "house-church" reflects how Catholics would gather in secret before the legalization of Christianity in 313. The Dura-Europos house-church is adorned with paintings of Adam and Eve, David and Goliath, and Christ as the Good Shepherd.

14

The first imperial-wide persecution of Christians did not occur until the third century

In A.D. 249, Emperor Decius wished to restore the Roman golden age and issued the first ever imperial-wide decree ordering the persecution of all those who refused to worship the Roman deities. The decree didn't target Christians exclusively, but it did mark the first time that the Christian faithful would have to choose publicly between worshipping the one true God or the emperor and all the gods and goddesses he established for worship. Another imperial-wide persecution broke out again in A.D. 303 under Emperor Diocletian, lasting intermittently until Constantine signed the Edict of Milan in 313.

"All who denied that they were or had been Christians, I discharged because they called upon the gods at my dictation and did reverence with wine and incense to your sacred image . . . and especially because they cursed Christ, a thing which—it is said— genuine Christians can in no way be induced to do."

–PLINY THE YOUNGER TO THE EMPEROR TRAJAN, LETTER 10

(*top*) Aureus (obverse) of Trajan Decius (249-251) draped, wearing a laurel wreath (gold) Inscription: IMP TRAIANVS DECIVS AVG, Roman, (3rd century A.D.) / Private Collection / Bridgeman Images. (*bottom*) Aureus (obverse) of Diocletian (A.D. 284-A.D. 305) cuirassed, wearing a laurel wreath. (gold), Inscription: IMP C C VAL DIOCLETIANVS P F AVG Roman, (4th century A.D.) / Private Collection / Bridgeman Images

Origen of Alexandria is considered both an important Christian teacher and a heretic

The first real systematic thinker of Christian theology was Origen of Alexandria (d. 254). His writings were controversial, including his belief that the Holy Trinity was hierarchical rather than consisting of equality between the Father, Son, and Holy Spirit. Origen also believed that all souls, even Satan, could eventually be saved, a theory called apocatastasis. Three centuries after his death, the Second Council of Constantinople pronounced him a heretic: "Whoever says or thinks that the punishment of demons and the wicked will not be eternal... let him be anathema." Despite this condemnation, Origen created hundreds of important works for the Church, and some twentieth-century theologians feel that he was misunderstood, and thus maligned.

(right) Origen, Illustration from "Les Vrais Portraits Et Vies Des Hommes Illustres" by André Thévet. Public domain via Wikimedia Commons.

16 Emperor Constantine legalized Christianity

In 306, the young Constantine was made a co-emperor and began a long trek from Britain, through Gaul, and into Italy to defeat his rival Maxentius to claim sole imperial power. The night before the battle at the Milvian Bridge outside Rome in October 312, Constantine had a vision in which Jesus instructed him to adorn the shields of his soldiers with the Chi-Rho symbol, shorthand for the word Christ. Another version of the story tells that

Constantine heard the message, *In Hoc Signo Vinces*, meaning, "In this Sign You Will Conquer." Constantine obeyed the directions given in the vision, and after emerging victorious in battle, prohibited further persecutions of Christians. He issued the Edict of Milan in 313 that granted the Church legal standing, thus putting an end to Christian persecution in the Roman Empire.

(*above*) The Emperor Constantine seeing a vision in the sky before the Battle of the Milvian Bridge in 312, which began his conversion to Christianity. The vision of Constantine (chromolitho), French School, (19th century) / Private Collection / © Look and Learn / Bridgeman Images. (*opposite*) The Baptism of Constantine, (oil on canvas), Vanni, Francesco (1563-1610) / Mondadori Portfolio/Electa/Foto Grassi / Bridgeman Images.

17 The age of martyrdom gave way to the age of monasticism

After the Edict of Milan, Christ's Church experienced an age of freedom they had never seen before. This newfound liberty brought an end to the age of the martyrs and gave way to the age of the monks. Christian ascetics left the cities to go to the deserts in Egypt and Mesopotamia to wage war with the devil. These were the new heroes and heroines, and legends of them abounded. The most popular account is the life of St. Anthony of Egypt, who, after hearing a local priest proclaim Matthew's injunction to seek perfection by selling all one has (see Mt 19:21), left everything behind and went to the desert near the Red Sea where he lived in consecrated solitude.

(*above*) Temptation of St. Anthony, 1510-1515, detail from panel of Isenheim altarpiece, by Matthias Grunewald (circa 1470-1530) / De Agostini Picture Library / G. Dagli Orti / Bridgeman Images

(*above*) The First Council of Nicaea. Fresco in Capella Sistina, Vatican. 1590. Public domain via Wikimedia Commons.

Heresy often helped clarify Church teaching

18

Emperor Constantine summoned all the Christian bishops in the city of Nicaea (modern-day Turkey) in the year 325. The first ecumenical council was held to address the heresy of Arianism. Arius, a priest in Alexandria, tried to maintain that the Son was not divine or one in substance with the Father. This is why Christians profess the *consubstantiality* of the Son and the Father in the Nicene Creed during Mass.

I believe in one Lord Jesus Christ,
the Only Begotten Son of God,
born of the Father before all ages.
God from God, Light from Light,
true God from true God,
begotten, not made, consubstantial with the Father;
through him all things were made.
For us men and for our salvation
he came down from heaven,
and by the Holy Spirit was incarnate of the Virgin Mary,
and became man.

—NICENE CREED

19 The Catholic Church gave us the Bible

The Catholic Church trusted the Holy Spirit to select which books belonged in the Bible and which ones did not. This process was called the canonization (*kanon*, Greek for "measuring stick"). With prayer, study, and the gift of communal discernment, bishops in the fourth and fifth centuries had to determine which books were truly inspired by God versus which ones were of merely human origin. In later times, the term canonization was also applied to the process of determining a person's potential sainthood.

The Holy Bible has always consisted of seventy-three books

20

In the sixteenth century, the reformer Martin Luther removed seven books from the Old Testament—Judith, Tobit, Wisdom, 1 and 2 Maccabees, Sirach, Baruch, and various portions of Daniel and Esther—and attempted to do away with parts of the New Testament, namely the Letter to James and the Book of Revelation. This is why the Catholic Bible is much older and contains seven more books that Catholics call deuterocanonical and Protestants call apocryphal.

21 False prophets claimed to have written divinely inspired gospels

Many false prophets composed their own gospels, attempting to pass them off as authoritative—the gospel of Judas, the gospel of Peter, and the gospel of Thomas were all presented as divinely inspired. The Church, however, proclaimed only four canonical Gospels—Matthew, Mark, Luke, and John—in the chronological order they were believed to have been written. The early Christians saw in these four Gospels the four creatures of the vision of the Prophet Ezekiel (see Ez 1:10) and reflected in the Book of Revelation (see Rev 4:7): a winged man, a lion, an ox, and an eagle.

22 Christianity put the Olympics on hold

When the Edict of Thessalonica made Christianity the official religion of the Roman Empire in the year 380, Emperor Theodosius eliminated many holdover pagan practices, including animal sacrifices, haruspicy (reading animal entrails), and divination (fortune telling). Theodosius also eliminated the Olympic games in Greece because of the worship of Greek gods and goddesses associated with the games. The Olympic games didn't resume until 1896.

(*above*) Panathenaic black figure amphora depicting a foot race (pottery), Greek, (5th century BC) / Musee Municipal Antoine Vivenel, Compiegne, France / Bridgeman Images. (*opposite*) Vision of Ezekiel, c.1518 (oil on panel), Raphael (Raffaello Sanzio of Urbino) (1483-1520) / Palazzo Pitti, Florence, Italy / Bridgeman Images

(*above*) The Four Doctors of the Western Church: Saint Jerome / Kingston Lacy, Dorset, UK / National Trust Photographic Library / Bridgeman Images.

23 Saint Jerome's Vulgate shifted the language of Christianity from Greek to Latin

In 384, the monk and learned polyglot Jerome was asked by Pope Damasus to compile an authoritative Latin text of Scripture and to help him regularize the sacred liturgy into Latin. Up until this point Christianity was a religion that used Greek. Jerome's Vulgate (from *vulgus* meaning "common," or "accessible for the people") was a groundbreaking Latin translation in its faithfulness to the Hebrew of the Old Testament, and the Greek of the New.

The First Council of Constantinople declared the divinity of the Holy Spirit

24

The First Council of Constantinople was held in 381 in order to, among other things, address the divinity of the Holy Spirit. A heretical group known as the followers of Macedonius, or the Pneumatomachi (from Greek for "Spirit Fighters"), contested the divinity of the Holy Spirit, compelling the bishops gathered at Constantinople to make the following addition to the Nicene Creed: "the Lord and Giver of Life, who proceeds from the Father, who with the Father and Son is adored and glorified, who has spoken through the prophets." In 589, the statement that the Spirit proceeds from the Father *and the Son* had to be clarified at the Third Council of Toledo.

(*Left*) Emperor Theodosius I at the Council of Costantinople, Latin manuscript, Turkey 9th Century / De Agostini Picture Library / A. Dagli Orti / Bridgeman Images. (*Right*) Council of Constantinople: blaze of heretical Macedonian books, miniature from manuscript 165, Italy 9th Century / De Agostini Picture Library / A. Dagli Orti / Bridgeman Images.

25 One fourth-century family produced six saints

I n the fourth century, a family in central Turkey gave rise to a pair of grandparents, a mother, one daughter, and two brothers who all became saints. Two important early theologians came from this family: Basil the Great and his brother Gregory of Nyssa. They both had pivotal roles in developing the Church's teaching on the divinity of the Holy Spirit and Christian holiness. Basil and Gregory also had a sister, Macrina the Younger, who was a formidable theologian in her own right. These three and their mother, Emmelia of Caesarea, are all saints in the Eastern Rite. Their grandfather was locally venerated as an early Christian martyr and their grandmother was St. Macrina the Elder.

(*left and right*) St. Gregory of Nyssa and St. Basil Great, fathers of the Greek Orthodox Church, engraving, 4th century / Bibliotheque des Arts Decoratifs, Paris, France / De Agostini Picture Library / Bridgeman Imageses.

(*above*) Patients and nuns at the Hospital of Hotel Dieu in Paris, from 'Le Livre de Vie Active de l'Hotel Dieu' by Jean Henry, c.1482 (vellum), French School, (15th century) / Musee de l'Assistance Publique, Hopitaux de Paris, France / Archives Charmet / Bridgeman Images

Hospitals have their roots in Christianity

26

The Romans did not want the ailing and the lame congregating in their cities. Some Christian doctors, like St. Cyrus and St. John, were even martyred for taking care of the sick. But when Christianity was finally legalized, nearly every major town with a bishop's cathedral was also expected to have a hospital. These early hospitals were originally called *basilias*, named after St. Basil the Great because of his efforts to establish health centers throughout the empire. Not only were the sick treated at the *basilias*, but these early hospitals were also places where medical courses were conducted, libraries maintained, and medicine distributed free of charge. The first known professionally trained nurses were actually religious sisters from the Daughters of Charity of St. Vincent de Paul, dating back to 1633. Today in the U.S. alone, Catholic hospitals serve nearly eighty million people annually as well as ninety-eight million outpatients, and account for 15 percent of all admissions.

But whom do we harm by building a place of caring for strangers, both for those who are on a journey and for those who require medical treatment on account of sickness, and so establishing a means of giving these men the comfort they deserve, physicians, doctors, means of conveyance, and escort?

—ST. BASIL'S LETTER 94 TO ELIAS, GOVERNOR OF THE ASIAN PROVINCE

27 The Council of Ephesus defined Mary as Theotókos

In 431, approximately 250 bishops led by St. Cyril of Alexandria were convened by Emperor Theodosius II to address the powerful and persuasive archbishop of Constantinople, Nestorius, who refused to allow his congregants to invoke Mary as the Mother of God. Nestorius argued that a creature could only be the mother of a creature, so Mary could not be the mother of Jesus's divinity, but only of His humanity. In response, the Council of Ephesus condemned him and upheld the ancient Christian practice of invoking Mary as *Mater Dei* (Mother of God), or *Theotókos* (God-bearer).

(*right*) Virgin and Child, 1888 (oil on canvas), Bouguereau, William-Adolphe (1825-1905) / Art Gallery of South Australia, Adelaide, Australia / Bridgeman Images

The Church declared Jesus's two natures as unchanged, unconfused, indivisible, and inseparable

Around 451, a group led by a charismatic monk named Eutyches asserted that Christ's divinity far outweighed His humanity, leaving Him essentially with only one nature. Pope Leo wrote a famous letter, called the *The Tome*, to condemn these Monophysites for refusing to uphold the Council of Chalcedon's definition of how the two natures of Jesus Christ are to be understood. The Church thus declared that the two natures of Jesus Christ are always and everywhere:

(*above*) Pope Leo I, Herrera, Francisco (1576-1656) / Prado, Madrid, Spain / Bridgeman Images

UNCHANGED	divinity does not change into humanity and vice-versa
UNCONFUSED	in Christ, humanity and divinity remain distinct and do not mingle into a new third nature
INDIVISIBLE	Jesus is never to be understood as two distinct individuals
INSEPARABLE	one can never say at some times only Jesus's human nature acts and at other times only His divine nature operates apart from His humanity

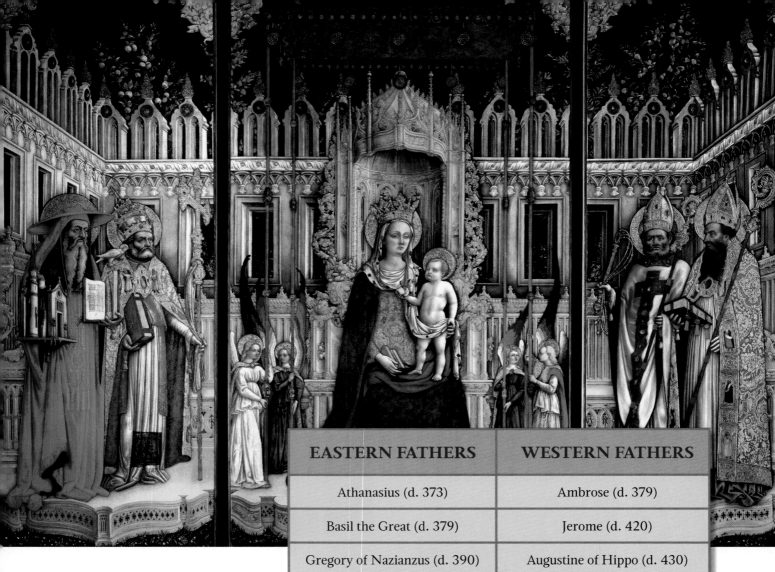

EASTERN FATHERS	WESTERN FATHERS
Athanasius (d. 373)	Ambrose (d. 379)
Basil the Great (d. 379)	Jerome (d. 420)
Gregory of Nazianzus (d. 390)	Augustine of Hippo (d. 430)
John Chrysostom (d. 407)	Gregory the Great (d. 604)

29

There are Eight Great Church Fathers

Over the centuries, the Church has proclaimed Eight Great Church Fathers, four in the West and four in the East. These figures are foundational because they shaped the Christian conversation in how we have come to think about God, salvation, and the Church's role in the world. St. Augustine is arguably the most influential of the group, leaving us almost five and a half million words to learn from and meditate upon.

The practice of venerating relics dates back to the second century

One night, as the soldier Martin of Tours was returning to the city of Amiens, France, he saw a shabbily dressed beggar. Moved with pity, Martin removed his cape and cleaved it in two with his sword, giving one half to the shivering homeless man. That night in a dream he saw Christ clad in the cloak he had torn and realized that the beggar was the Lord Himself. Martin's robe was later miraculously restored and put on display to be venerated in what would eventually be called a chapel (capella), derived from the word cape (cappa). There is evidence of similar reliquaries and ossuaries holding other items of saints, even their hair and bones, as early as the second century. While sometimes foreign to the modern mind, this practice of praying with relics reminds us that the divine became flesh and that God continues to draw near to His faithful through the flesh of His saints.

(*right*) Relic of Saint John Bosco. Blessing of Saint John Bosco Church, Maribo. Photo public domain via Wikimedia Commons.

31 St. Benedict founded Western Monasticism

Soon after the fall of the Roman Empire, Benedict of Nursia created his monumental Rule in 529, the first real guidebook to institutionalize monastic life. Converting a pagan temple into a Christian monastery in Nursia, Benedict gathered together two brothers who wanted to live a common, Christocentric life. Benedict's Rule was groundbreaking in that it fostered prudence and humanity, providing both spiritual and administrative guidance.

"Listen, O my son, to the precepts of thy master, and incline the ear of thy heart, and cheerfully receive and faithfully execute the admonitions of thy loving Father, that by the toil of obedience thou mayest return to Him from whom by the sloth of disobedience thou hast gone away."

—OPENING PROLOGUE TO BENEDICT'S RULE

(*left*) Ms. 197 f.1r Rule of St. Benedict (vellum), English School, (10th century) / © Corpus Christi College, Oxford, UK / Bridgeman Images

(*above*) Benedictine Monks, from the Life of St. Benedict (fresco) (detail), Signorelli, L. (c.1441-1523) & Sodoma, G. (1477-1549) / Monte Oliveto Maggiore, Tuscany, Italy / Bridgeman Images

Due to a papal decree, the days between October 4 and October 15 in the year 1582 never happened

32

In 1582, Pope Gregory XIII issued a papal bull ordering a reform of the old Julian calendar. As intelligent as the Romans were, the sun proved faster than their calendar, and Caesar's 365-day year was eleven minutes and ten seconds too long, so that by 1582 the old calendar was more than ten days behind. The pope employed two prominent astronomers to calculate the true length of the year, which gave rise to the pope's new Gregorian calendar. To catch up to the new calendar, Gregory jumped ahead ten days so that October 4 instantly became October 15, 1582.

33 Two men are credited with the terms "before Christ" and "anno Domini"

A desert monk named Dionysius was the first to designate Jesus's birth as the year 0, thus giving rise to the new demarcation of A.D. (*anno Domini*), in the year of our Lord. In 731, Venerable Bede was the first historian to refer to the years *before Christ*, and eventually the abbreviation B.C. became standard with the rise of the English language.

Charlemagne was the first Holy Roman emperor

On Christmas Day in the year 800, Pope Leo III waited in the back of St. Peter's Basilica for King Charles to enter for Holy Mass. At this Mass, the pope would crown Charles the Great (Charlemagne) as the first emperor of the Holy Roman Empire. Hailed as another Constantine, Charlemagne fought for the Church's rights, led his armies into Muslim-taken Spain, and sought to reform the clergy and the people of his lands. Charlemagne's reforms focused on the renewal of art, literature, history, and architecture, so that this time period eventually become known as the Carolingian Renaissance.

(*above*) Charlemagne (747-814) crowned King of Italy in 774 (oil on canvas), French School, (19th century) / Château de Versailles, France / Index / Bridgeman Images

35 A pope's corpse was exhumed and put on trial at the Cadaver Synod

Distrustful of Emperor Guy III of Spoleto and his son Lambert, Pope Formosus crowned Arnulf of Carinthia as lawful emperor. Formosus would later convince Arnulf to attack Lambert in battle, but Arnulf failed. Soon after this, Pope Formosus died, leaving Lambert to rule single-handedly. Lambert then forced Pope Stephen VI to accuse his predecessor of political treason. The Cadaver Synod was thus convened. In January 897, the corpse of Pope Formosus was exhumed from the Vatican graveyard, vested in papal regalia, and put on trial at St. John Lateran's Basilica. Not surprisingly, he was found guilty on all accounts, and parts of his remains were dumped unceremoniously into the Tiber River.

(*above*) Pope Formosus and Stephen VI (oil on canvas). Laurens, Jean-Paul. 1870. Public doman via Wikimedia Commons.

(*above*) Saints Cyril and Methodius, fresco by unknown artist, in Markos monastery, 1346, Markova Susica, Macedonia, 14th century / De Agostini Picture Library / Bridgeman Images

Catholic missionaries helped shape many languages

36

Over the centuries, popes sent missionaries to all corners of the world to teach and spread the gospel. Saints Cyril and Methodius not only converted the Slavs but were also helpful in creating the Cyrillic alphabet. Dominican Father James Kyushei Tomonaga composed one of the first modern Japanese grammars and dictionaries; Jesuit Saint Jose de Anchieta is the Father of Brazilian literature; Alexandre de Rhodes was the first to translate the Vietnamese language into Roman characters; and the first item ever printed in Wisconsin was a liturgical calendar in the language of the Chippewa Indians in 1834 by Fr. Samuel Mazzuchelli.

37 The Great Schism separated Roman Catholic and Eastern Orthodox rites

In 1054, Pope Leo IX insisted that Rome's claim to be the Head and Mother of all Churches be recognized. Not only did Patriarch Michael Cerularius in Constantinople refuse, he excommunicated the legates and was in turn excommunicated himself. Eastern bishops condemned the addition of the Filioque clause to the Nicene-Constantinpolitan Creed, which they judged as an illicit incursion upon their autonomy by the West. With a new desire for reunion expressed at the Second Vatican Council, Pope Paul VI and the Orthodox Patriarch, Athenagoras, lifted the mutual excommunications and issued a Catholic-Orthodox Joint Declaration in 1965.

(*below*) The Beautiful Hagia Sofia in Istanbul. Photo © klempa / Shutterstock.

(*above*) Pope Gregory XV and Cardinal Ludovisi declaring canonization of St. Ignatius of Loyola and St. Francis Xavier, painting by unknown artist, Church of Gesu, Rome, Italy, 17th century / De Agostini Picture Library / G. Dagli Orti / Bridgeman Images

"The Devil's Advocate" was (and still is) a real position in the Church

38

In the very early days of Christianity, a local community would recognize someone as a saint after his death, holding him up as a person who lived an exemplary and heroic life for Jesus. Beginning around 1000, however, the Church desired greater uniformity and scrutiny, so both bishops and popes began to regularize this process. To better authenticate the canonization, the Church even devised a position known as "the Devil's Advocate" in 1450. This person's job was to cast doubt on the virtues and miracles reported when a holy man or woman was brought to the pope to be recognized as a saint. This position still exists today.

(*above*) Photo © L'osservatore Romano

39 The papal conclave was created to hasten the election of a new pope

Roman cardinals have had the exclusive right of selecting popes since 1059. Early cardinals came mainly from Rome and nearby dioceses, but today's cardinals represent various national-

ities. Due to delays in electing popes, Pope Gregory X decreed in 1274 that the cardinals should be locked away until they settled on a candidate. Thus conclave essentially means to be "locked up."

The Crusades were launched to reclaim Christian lands

When the Prophet Mohammed founded Islam, it was inevitable that Christians, Jews, and Muslims would eventually battle over land and resources. For centuries, Muslims conquered and killed Christians from Mecca eastward into Asia Minor, down through North Africa, and up into parts of Spain and southern France. When Pope Urban called for the First Crusade in 1095, almost two-thirds of Christian lands were ruled by Muslim leaders. Between 1095 and 1272, the Church sponsored seven or nine official crusades (depending on how one chooses to categorize a crusade), while other, more sporadic attempts to recover Christian lands and holy sites occurred more frequently but much less systematically.

(*below*) Taking of Jerusalem by the Crusaders, 15th July 1099, 1847 (oil on canvas), Signol, Emile (1804-92) / Château de Versailles, France / Bridgeman Images

41 The legend of the female "Pope Joan" has no validity

Over the millennia, the papacy has survived many propagandist attacks, and the story of a "Pope Joan" may have been the first, dating back to a tall tale written around 1250. A Dominican, Martin of Opova, invented a story of a ninth-century female pope who supposedly lived as a man named John Anglicus of Mainz. As the story goes, "John" entered the seminary and was eventually elected pope, only to be found a woman when she gave birth during a solemn liturgical procession. As fanciful as such a story is, some see in it a retelling of one of the most powerful women the Church has known—Marozia Theophylact—who was the mistress of one pope, the mother of another, and the possible assassin of a third. No matter the source of the story, there is no official record of a female pope.

(*below*) Pope Joan giving birth. Woodcut from a German translation by Heinrich Steinhöwel of Giovanni Boccaccio's De mulieribus claris, printed by Johannes Zainer at Ulm ca. 1474 (British Museum). Public domain via Wikimedia Commons.

IOHANNES·PAPA

(*above*) Henry IV (1050-1106), King of Germany from 1056 and Holy Roman emperor from 1084, doing penance at Pope Hildebrand's Gate., illustration from 'The History of Protestantism' by James Aitken Wylie (1808-1890), pub. 1878 (engraving), English School, (19th century) / Private Collection / The Stapleton Collection / Bridgeman Images

The Concordat of Worms settled the Investiture Controversy

42

The most significant clash between the empire and the Church was the Investiture Controversy of the eleventh and twelfth centuries. At stake was who held the rightful power to appoint bishops and abbots of major monasteries—the pope or the ruling monarch of the land. This conflict of powers began with Pope St. Gregory VII, who initiated major clerical reforms, and ended in 1122 when Pope Calixtus II met with the Holy Roman emperor Henry V at the Concordat of Worms where the rightful division of spiritual from temporal power was agreed upon. Despite inevitable power struggles between monarch and pope in subsequent centuries, it was settled that no temporal ruler had the right to control the Church's elections of bishops and abbots. Canonical elections and consecrations were now squarely under the jurisdiction of the pope and metropolitan bishops.

(*above*) Exterior view of the Cistercian Abbey (photo), French School, (11th century) / Cîteaux, France / Bridgeman Images. (*right*) Crozier of St. Robert, c.1100 (gilded silver), French School, (12th century) / Musee des Beaux-Arts, Dijon, France / Bridgeman Images

43 Cistercian monks helped form Christian civilizations

In 1098, a monk and twenty-one brothers from the famous and rapidly expanding monastery of Molesme left in search of a more austere way of life. Robert of Molesme, the English monk, Stephen Harding, St. Alberic, and a handful of others founded the Cistercians, named after the local city of Cîteaux. They emphasized manual labor as a source of income rather than feudal revenues.

Throughout the years, the Cistercians flourished and from them came the Trappists, or the Cistercians of the Strict Observance (OCSO). Such groups like these considered farming their chief occupation and developed new agricultural techniques. They transformed Europe and were instrumental in forming and transmitting Christian culture.

St. Anselm is the father of Scholasticism

With his writings, St. Anselm of Canterbury introduced a new way of theologizing. Called the Father of Scholasticism, Anselm, a Benedictine monk elected bishop of Canterbury, helped establish reason, and not simply biblical authority, as the basis for belief in God. Anselm wanted Christians to understand the rationality of their own faith, and he thought philosophy was a non-threatening tool with which he could appeal to non-believers as well. His ontological proof concerning the existence of God and the satisfaction theory of atonement were some of his most famous concepts. Anselm was also among the first to parallel Mary's motherhood with God's fatherhood.

(*above*) William II conferring the primacy on Anselm, 1093 (colour litho), Herbert, Sydney (1854-1914) / Private Collection / © Look and Learn / Bridgeman Images.

(*above*) One of the most celebrated pieces of English medieval music blending secular melody with sacred text; tune called Perspice Christicola. The earliest example of ground-bass. Produced at Reading Abbey, (vellum), English School, (13th century) / British Library, London, UK / © British Library Board. All Rights Reserved / Bridgeman Images. (*right*) One of the three known portraits of Antonio Vivaldi (oil on canvas), Italian School, (18th century) / Civico Museo Bibliografico Musicale, Bologna, Italy / Bridgeman Images.

45

The Church is one of the most notable patrons of music

While Bishop Ambrose was innovative in introducing various melodies into the Mass in fourth century Milan, the most famous form of chant—Gregorian—takes its name from Pope Gregory the Great. Meanwhile, a Benedictine monk named Guido of Arezzo invented staff notation to assist his brothers in the understanding and execution of Gregorian chant. This Christian love of harmony continued from there, as one of the greatest baroque composers was not only a pioneer in classical music but also a Catholic priest. Antonio Vivaldi, best known as the composer of The Four Seasons, was ordained in Venice, and as part of his outreach to the poor, wrote music to be performed for the Hospital of Mercy, a home for abandoned children in Venice where Vivaldi worked.

The Church has patron saints for headaches, ugliness, fireworks, hangovers, and television

The Church has canonized many saints who fill all sorts of patron roles. St. Drogo was a virtuous orphan from Flanders who became hideously afflicted with a terrible skin disease. He was forced to live in seclusion because of his disfigurement, but word of his holiness spread and people came to him for miraculous healings. Today he is known as the patron of ugly people. Another strange but wonderful saint is St. Barbara, the Patroness of Fireworks and of Artillerymen, who was beheaded by her husband after converting to Christianity. Shortly after killing his wife, he was struck dead by lightning. St. Denis is the Patron of Headache Sufferers because he did not like the place where his persecutors beheaded him, so he picked up his head and walked another six miles, preaching a sermon on martyrdom the whole way. St. Bibiana is the Patroness and kind intercessor of those who suffer from hangovers; while St. Clare of Assisi is the Patroness of Television due to her ability to bi-locate, and thus be at many places at once.

(*right*) Statue of Saint Denis beheaded, patron and first bishop of Paris, in the Crypte of the Sacre Coeur. Photo © Jose Ignacio Soto / Shutterstock.

47 The teachings of Aristotle were integral to shaping Catholic thought

Nearly all of Aristotle's works were translated into Latin between 1150 and 1250. This new source of human wisdom caused a revolution in learning and the scholastic method began. Great thinkers like the Dominicans Albert the Great and his student Thomas Aquinas found in Aristotle's metaphysics, politics, and ethics new and exciting ways to explain the ancient truths of the Christian faith. The most impressive synthesis of Aristotelian reason and Catholic revelation was Thomas Aquinas's well-known work, *Summa Theologiae.*

(*above*) Apotheosis of St. Thomas Aquinas by, Francesco Traini (active 1321-1345), tempera and gold on wood, 375x258 cm, from Church of Santa Caterina, Pisa / De Agostini Picture Library / G. Nimatallah / Bridgeman Images

(*above*) St. Dominic and his Companions Fed by Angels, from the predella panel of the Coronation of the Virgin, c.1430-32 (tempera on panel), Angelico, Fra (Guido di Pietro) (c.1387-1455) / Louvre, Paris, France / Bridgeman Images

Monastic orders became everyday fixtures throughout thirteenth century Europe

48

While monastic groups like the Benedictines and Cistercians continued to thrive in the Church, groups focusing more on communal poverty and preaching well beyond the monastery walls came into existence. In fact, the Second Council of Lyon officially recognized four new orders: the Franciscans, the Dominicans, the Carmelites, and the Augustinians. While each of these groups arose to meet various needs and challenges, their founding saints, specifically Dominic and Francis, became the new bellwethers of the Church's expansion. Friars and sisters became standard fixtures in the growing urban centers of Europe, extending a monastic zeal out into the everyday lives of all Christians.

49

The Church was a major proponent of scientific advancement

The Catholic Church has been accused of having a hostile relationship with science, but scientific breakthroughs often came from the Church's greatest minds. St. Albert the Great was one of the forerunners of modern science and was even said to have constructed a medieval robot that moved and spoke. Other scientific achievements within the Church included the invention of the electric motor by Andrew Gordon, a Benedictine monk, and the co-invention of the internal combustion engine by the Italian Piarist Father Eugenio Barsanti.

(*above*) God as Architect/Builder/Geometer/ Craftsman, The Frontispiece of Bible Moralisee (illumination on parchment) 1220-1230. Austrian National Library. Public domain via Wikimedia Commons

50

Dante composed one of the most famous poems ever written

Dante of Alighieri was a Catholic Italian poet who composed an epic poem, titled the Divine Comedy, depicting a journey through the afterlife, beginning in hell, working up through purgatory, and ending in heaven. His haunting depictions and symbolic depth drew millions of readers to his work and inspired countless forms of art and other literature. Over seven centuries later, people still reference the Divine Comedy in popular culture, both Catholic and secular alike.

51 Seven popes resided in France instead of Rome

Distressed by corruption and political scheming in Rome, Pope Clement V moved the papacy from the Vatican Hill to Avignon, France in 1309. The next seven popes were French and the Avignon papacy remained firm for nearly seventy years. St. Catherine of Siena successfully appealed to the last of the Avignon popes, Gregory XI, to end the "Babylonian Captivity" of Christ's papacy. He returned the papacy to Rome in 1377 and, in many ways, this "happy fault" of temporary exile brought about positive changes, including the reorganization of curial structures, the educational reform amongst the clergy, and a greater attention to how political power sways papal actions.

(*below*) Palais des Papes (Papal Palace), Avignon, France. Photo © Dreamer Company / Shutterstock.

Three men claimed to be pope at once

Politics and theological disagreements created the Western Schism in which three men claimed the papacy as their own. After Pope Gregory XI returned the papacy to Rome, factions continued to follow the bishop of Avignon as the legitimate successor. From 1378 to 1414, the "papal schism" resulted in a total of seven anti-popes claiming primacy in both Avignon and Rome. The confusion continued until anti-pope John XXIII convened the Council of Constance at the insistence of Emperor Sigismund, who demanded ecclesiastical unity. At Constance, Gregory XII, Benedict XIII, and John XXIII all abdicated, and a Roman, Martin V, was elected. The actions at Constance echoed through the centuries, giving rise to the theological position of Conciliarism: the idea that supreme authority is to be found in a general council of bishops rather than in any single pope.

(*left*) Antipope Benedict XIII (b/w photo) / © SZ Photo / Bridgeman Images. (*middle*) Antipope John XXIII, 1410–1415 (b/w photo) / © SZ Photo / Scherl / Bridgeman Images. (*right*) Gregory XII. Pope between 1406 and 1415. Engraving. / Photo © Tarker / Bridgeman Images.

Joan of Arc is known as the Maid of Orléans

The Hundred Years' War raged from 1337 to 1452 as the English House of Plantagenet sought sovereignty in France against the House of Valois. Saying she was sent by Michael the Archangel and Catherine of Siena, young Joan of Arc presented herself to King Charles VII who sent her into Orléans as part of a relief mission. Brave but inexperienced in battle, Joan was captured by the English, placed on trial, and condemned as both a political enemy and a Catholic heretic. With a self-appointed tribunal, the English predictably found nineteen-year-old Joan guilty on all charges, sentencing her to the flames on May 30, 1431. Twenty years later, Pope Callixtus III officially exonerated her and held her up as a faithful daughter of both France and the Church. Joan became known as the Maid of Orléans (*maid* is old English for "virgin") and was canonized by Pope Benedict XV in 1920.

(*above*) The Peasant Maid of Orleans in the Hands of the English, illustration from 'Hutchinson's History of the British Nation' (colour litho) c. 1920, Wheelwright, Roland (1870-1955) (after) / Private Collection / Bridgeman Images

54 There are seven sins that lead to excommunication

Excommunication from the Church has its roots in Scripture (see Lv 18:29, Mt 18:15–18, 1 Cor 5:1–8). While various offenses can distance any individual from receiving Communion, the 1983 Code of Canon Law lists the following seven sins as reasons for automatic sentence of excommunication:

1. When one publicly apostatizes (renounces) the Catholic faith
2. When one intentionally desecrates the Most Holy Eucharist
3. When one commits bodily violence against the pope
4. When a confessor uses the seal of confession to solicit a penitent for sinful acts
5. When a bishop consecrates another bishop without direct papal permission
6. When a confessor willingly breaks the "seal" or secrecy of what was told to him in confession during the Sacrament of Reconciliation
7. When one cooperates in the aborting of an unborn child

(*above*) Saint Ambrose, Bishop of Milan, Refusing Emperor Theodosius Admission to Milan Cathedral (oil on canvas), Boeyermans, Theodor (1620-78) / Private Collection / Photo © Christie's Images / Bridgeman Images

(*above*) The Expulsion of the Jews from Spain, from 'Hutchinson's History of the Nations' (colour litho), Hart, Solomon Alexander (1806-81) / Private Collection / Bridgeman Images

The Spanish Inquisition was only one of many inquisitions

55

The Church established an office of Inquisition in 1184 to look into heretical sects and cults endangering Christian unity. Some of these inquisitions, including the Medieval or Papal Inquisition, must be distinguished from the more notorious Spanish Inquisition that, sadly, still had laws in effect until 1834. Later in history, in 1908, the Roman Inquisition became the "Sacred Congregation of the Holy Office" before changing again during Vatican II to the "Congregation for the Doctrine of the Faith," directed most notably by Joseph Ratzinger. Despite the harmful consequences of the Spanish Inquisition, other inquisitions in Church history were necessary and helped protect the Church from error and division.

(*above*) Gutenberg inventing printing press (1773-1832), Laurent, Jean Antoine (1763-1832) / Musee de Grenoble, France / De Agostini Picture Library / G. Dagli Orti / Bridgeman Images. (right) Johann Gutenberg's (1400-1468) first printing press. Engraving published Mainz 1856. / Universal History Archive/ UIG / Bridgeman Images.

56 The Holy Bible was the first work of the Gutenberg Press

Before the invention of moveable type, few people outside a parish or monastery owned a Bible. But a German Catholic named Johannes Gutenberg revolutionized the way people would read and obtain information. His Gutenberg Press disseminated knowledge at an unprecedented rate and brought about an early form of globalization with the ability to print books quickly and relatively inexpensively. Gutenberg was sure to make the Bible his first printed work.

The fall of Constantinople brought about several positive repercussions

In 1453, the Byzantine Empire, essentially the continuation of the Eastern Roman Empire, came to an end when Constantinople was overrun by Muslim soldiers who renamed the city Istanbul. Christianity gave way to Islam and the Ottoman Empire was firmly established. But this caused many Byzantine scholars to flee to more friendly European countries, especially Italy, which provided the spark for the Renaissance and contributed to the Church's appropriation of not only Plato and Aristotle, but even many Jewish and Persian sources. Further, with Turkey now blocked off, more and more European efforts were put into commerce with China and the Far East. Finally, the Church in Russia took on a new identity as the "Third Rome," and Russian Orthodoxy enjoyed a new synthesis of classical wisdom and Christian learning.

(*above*) The Entry of Mahomet II into Constantinople (oil on canvas), Constant, Jean Joseph Benjamin (1845-1902) / Private Collection / Pictures from History / Bridgeman Images

(*above*) Luther in front of Cardinal Cajetan during the controversy of his 95 Theses, 1870 (oil on canvas), Pauwels, Ferdinand Wilhelm (1830-1904) / Lutherhaus, Eisenach, Germany / Bridgeman Images.

58 The Reformation didn't begin with Martin Luther

When the former Augustinian monk and priest Martin Luther nailed his Ninety-Five Theses to the cathedral door at Wittenberg in 1517, he did not really begin the Protestant Reformation. In reality, he joined a storm of resentment that had been brewing for over a century. Jan Hus had already convinced his followers, in what would become the Moravian Church, to abandon belief in the Real Presence of Christ in the Eucharist, while holding to an institutional Church, infant baptism, purgatory, and the need for good works.

The Lutheran Church made use of many of these staunchly Protestant tenets and built upon much of the theology aimed against Catholic disciplinary corruptions. A trained theologian and a gifted orator, Luther rallied crowds and convinced crowned rulers to break away from the Christianity of their youth. After heated exchanges with those sent from Rome to quell the tensions, Luther was excommunicated on January 3, 1521 by Pope Leo X. Lutheranism was born, and Christ's body was officially divided for the first time in the West.

King Henry VIII was once known as "Defender of the Faith"

Henry VIII earned the title "Defender of the Faith" as he defended the Catholic Church against Martin Luther's attacks. But soon after, the King turned on the Faith. To forge an alliance between the English Crown and Spain, Henry was betrothed to his deceased brother's wife, Catherine of Aragon (the first of his six wives). Having grown desirous of the younger Anne Boleyn, and hoping to have a male heir, he aimed to put Catherine away. When the English clergy forbad him, the King appointed Thomas Crammer as the new archbishop of Canterbury, and made himself the "Supreme Head of the Church of England" in his 1534 Act of Supremacy. Only St. John Fisher and St. Thomas More stood against him, and both were martyred. Thus, the Anglican Church was born.

(*below*) The Family of Henry VIII, c.1545 (oil on canvas), English School, (16th century) / Royal Collection Trust © Her Majesty Queen Elizabeth II, 2016 / Bridgeman Images

60 Various food and drink have their origins with the Church

The Church has developed many culinary delights. Cappuccino coffee takes its name from the brown habits of Capuchin Franciscans, while the famous French liqueur, Chartreuse, is the original recipe of Carthusian monks. The hops in beer first replaced grains thanks to French Benedictine Abbot Adalhard. Today, Trappist breweries still rank among the best in Europe. Speaking of alcohol, Dom Pérignon was a Benedictine monk who helped perfect the production of sparkling wines. Even pretzels have their origins in the Church, which first appeared in Italian monasteries in the seventh century. Named after *pretioloa*, they became little prizes for children who learned their prayers. It is said this is the reason the pretzel itself is made to look like two arms folded in prayer.

(*right*) Dom Perignon (1639-1715) Benedictine monk, inventor of the champagne, statue in Epernay, France / Photo © Tallandier / Bridgeman Images. (*above*) Pretzel. Photo © Igor Litvyak / Shutterstock.

John Calvin nearly became a priest

John Calvin was born in France and trained as a humanist in the best schools and universities. Originally destined for the priesthood, Calvin reacted strongly against Catholicism and abandoned the Church around 1530. Having grown reliant upon a rather skewed reading of St. Augustine's theology of grace, Calvin built his own theology based on the utter sovereignty of God and the total depravity of the human sinner. He accused Catholicism of being too reliant on man's initiative and essential goodness. Many of the Council of Trent's finer theological points were aimed against Calvinist principles.

(*right*) Portrait of Jean Calvin, 1858 (oil on canvas), Scheffer, Ary (1795-1858) / Musee de la Vie Romantique, Paris, France / Roger-Viollet, Paris / Bridgeman Images.

62 Catholicism inspired some of the world's greatest art

The central figures and mysteries of Christianity supplied images and motifs for some of the world's finest works of art. The Church has also given the world the best sculptors and painters. Michelangelo and his renowned Pietà as well as his famous scenes in the Sistine Chapel come immediately to mind. Other art legends include Giotto, Fra Angelico, Donatello, Titan, and Caravaggio, who all found their inspiration in the central truths of Christianity. The Gothic, Renaissance, and Baroque periods each began as efforts to inspire worship of God through the use of art.

(*above*) Pietà (marble), Buonarroti, Michelangelo (1475-1564), St. Peter's, Vatican City. Photo © Craig Mace / Saint Benedict Press. (*opposite*) Sistine Chapel ceiling and lunettes, 1508-12 (fresco) (post restoration), Buonarroti, Michelangelo (1475-1564) / Vatican Museums and Galleries, Vatican City / Bridgeman Images

(*above*) Miracle of St. Ignatius of Loyola, 1618-19, Peter Paul Rubens (1577-1640), oil on canvas / De Agostini Picture Library / G. Nimatallah / Bridgeman Images

63 The Jesuit founders helped bring the gospel to the corners of the earth

After being injured in the Battle of Pamplona, St. Ignatius of Loyola underwent a spiritual conversion. While recovering at his family's castle in Loyola, his weakness showed him the power of Christ and his desire to finally serve a king who would not die. During years of ascetic rigor and theological training, Ignatius composed the Spiritual Exercises, and while a student at the University of Paris,

he gathered like-minded men around him, including Francis Xavier and Peter Faber. These early companions professed private vows together in 1534, and by 1540 were formally recognized as the Society of Jesus (the Jesuits) by Pope Paul III. Within just a few years, over one thousand Jesuits had founded schools all over Europe and sent missionaries as far west as Canada and as far east as Japan.

The Protestant Reformation helped spark a spiritual revival in the Catholic Church

Pope Paul III called for an ecumenical council to address the Reformers' criticisms and to help cleanse the Church of corruption. From 1545 until 1563, bishops throughout Europe gathered at the northern Italian city of Trent, and at times in Bologna, because of civil unrest. Over these eighteen years, the Church produced some of her more formative documents and thoughts on the nature of the Church and the essential role of the sacraments in human sanctification, naturally paying special attention to those doctrines that were under attack by the Protestants, including original sin, the Sacraments of Baptism and Holy Eucharist, praying with relics and icons, purgatory, and the proper nature of indulgences. The Council of Trent marked the beginning of the Counter Reformation and sparked a spiritual revival in the Church.

(*above*) The First Chapter of the 25th Council of Trent, Venetian School, c.1630, Italian School, (17th century) / Phillips, The International Fine Art Auctioneers, UK / Photo © Bonhams, London, UK / Bridgeman Images

65 Sts. Teresa of Avila and John of the Cross were influential figures in the Counter Reformation

Two of the most influential Catholic reformers of the sixteenth century were the Carmelite saints Teresa of Avila and John of the Cross. Together, these two spearheaded a reform of their Carmelite communities so vast that it reverberated throughout other monastic orders as well. Teresa and John sought to reinstitute the Primitive Rule of 1209, restoring lengthier times for prayer, stricter mortifications, and a greater emphasis on material poverty. Carmelites today consist of many communities and continue to give the world saints worthy of selfless imitation, including Thérèse of Lisieux and the Jewish philosopher turned Christian martyr, Edith Stein.

O most beautiful flower of Mt. Carmel, fruitful vine, splendor of Heaven, Blessed Mother of the Son of God, Immaculate Virgin, assist me in my necessity. O Star of the Sea, help me and show me you are my Mother. O Holy Mary, Mother of God, Queen of Heaven and earth, I humbly beseech you from the bottom of my heart to succor me in this necessity (make request). There are none that can withstand your power. O Mary, conceived without sin, pray for us who have recourse to thee. Sweet Mother I place this cause in your hands. Amen.

—TRADITIONAL PRAYER TO OUR LADY OF MOUNT CARMEL

(*above*) Saint Teresa of Àvila Covering a Community of Carmelites with her Mantle / De Agostini Picture Library / G. Dagli Orti / Bridgeman Images

(*above*) The Vision of St. Philip Neri, 1721 (oil on canvas), Benefial, Marco (1684-1764) / Fitzwilliam Museum, University of Cambridge, UK / Bridgeman Images

St. Phillip Neri founded the Congregation of the Oratory

66

Another fruit of reform was the group of priests who gathered around the patron saint of joy and laughter, Philip Neri. Originally a group of young priests who came to serve the poor and sick in Rome, Neri and companions were officially recognized as the Congregation of the Oratory in 1575, spreading quickly into the rest of Europe. In 1611, Fr. Pierre de Bérulle founded the Oratory in Paris, and in 1848 John Henry Newman brought this new way of life into England. Oratorian spirituality is very Christocentric, stressing how Jesus Christ wishes to replicate his life in each of his followers, mystically living his life by extending his own incarnation in and through the life of every baptized Christian. The Congregation of the Oratory continues today, consisting of priests and lay-brothers who live together in a community bound by charity, rather than formal vows.

67 Many scholars believe Shakespeare was a Roman Catholic

Although he fulfilled the minimal requirements of Anglicanism to stay out of jail, contemporary scholars believe William Shakespeare was a devout Christian and possibly a Roman Catholic. His mother, Mary Arden, came from a faithful Catholic family, and there is a record of Shakespeare's father missing worship services in the Church of England. While Shakespeare's personal faith cannot be definitively proved, Catholic imagery and turns of phrases subversively abound throughout his 37 plays and 154 sonnets. Friars and priests appear often to save the day, the Church's sacraments are presented as channels of healing and transformation, Hamlet's murdered father speaks from purgatory, and the young religious Sister Isabella is the paragon of all Christian virtue in *Measure for Measure.*

A Third Order Dominican proposed the theory of heliocentricity before Galileo

Nicholas Copernicus (1473-1543) was a third order Dominican and a canon living at the Archcathedral Basilica of the Assumption in Frombork, Poland, when he composed some of his most significant treatises advancing a heliocentric theory of how the earth revolves around the sun. Such a view challenged scriptural passages, so Copernicus proceeded carefully, publishing important works at the request of high-rank-ing bishops and cardinals. Galileo Galilei later used the telescope to prove the Copernican Revolution, but lacked Copernicus' humility and piety, earning him the suspicion and even ire of Church officials. In 1633, Galileo was placed on trial and subsequently spent months under the equivalent of "house arrest," before returning to Florence. Saint John Paul II asked for public forgiveness for the Inquisition's hastiness in this matter and Pope Benedict commended Galileo for helping the whole Church "contemplate with gratitude God's works."

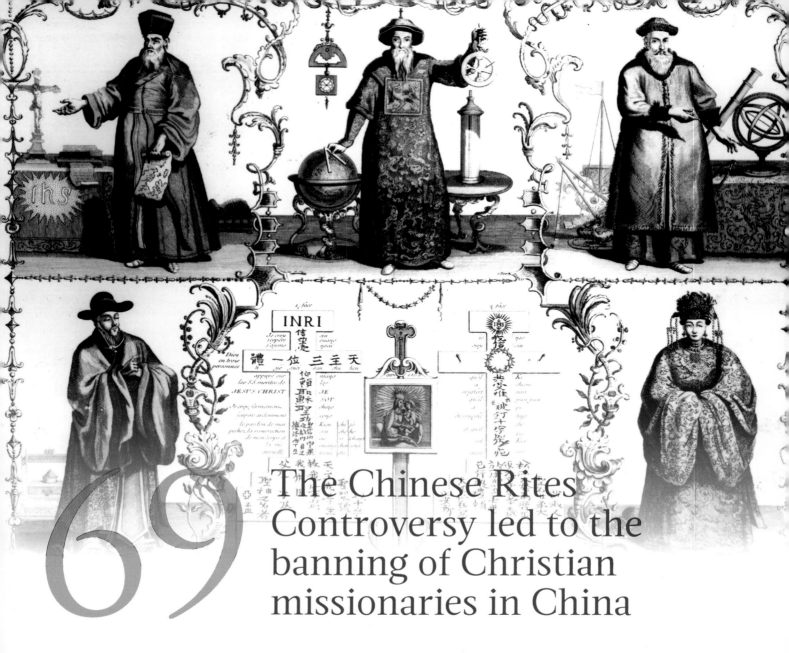

69 The Chinese Rites Controversy led to the banning of Christian missionaries in China

As missionaries flocked to the far corners of the globe, they often tried to reconcile cultural rituals to soften the dramatic change in a people's way of life that came from converting. As long as the rituals were not contrary to the gospel, they tried to find a way to let the people hold on to their traditions. This became complicated and ultimately brewed into controversy in China when Jesuit missionaries believed Chinese rites were native rituals perfectly compatible with Christianity. The Jesuits felt that, within certain limits,

their traditions could be tolerated. In what would become known as the Chinese Rites Controversy of 1715, Pope Clement XI condemned the Jesuits for allowing the Chinese people to retain certain elements of Confucianism and Buddhism, such as honoring their departed ancestors to the point of worship. The controversy led Chinese emperor to ban all Christian missions a few years later.

(*above*) The Jesuits in China (engraving), French School, (17th century) / Private Collection / Bridgeman Images.

France is considered the eldest daughter of the Church

France has always been intimately tied to the Catholic Church, earning her the nickname "the eldest daughter of the Church." This was never more apparent than during the Early Modern Period when devotions renewed the Church in France and a distinct spirituality of mystical union influenced preaching and prayers for centuries. Perhaps the best example of this was the Visitation Sister, Margaret Mary Alacoque, who experienced profound visions of Jesus's Sacred Heart. She gave rise to the popular devotion of meditating on Christ's pierced and loving heart. Additionally, St. Francis de Sales's *Introduction to the Devout Life* guided many laypeople in their pursuit of a joyful and practical Christianity; St. Vincent de Paul tirelessly founded religious congregations of men and women to work with children and the sick; and John Vianney became the patron of priests due to his tireless devotion to his people in Ars, making himself available for confession nearly sixteen hours each day.

(*above*) St. Francois de Sales (1567-1622) Giving the Rule of the Visitation to St. Jeanne de Chantal (1572-1641) (oil on canvas), Halle, Noel (1711-81) / Eglise Saint-Louis-en-L'Ile, Paris, France / Bridgeman Images

71 The Church influenced the abolition of slavery

Although many early Church Fathers saw the practice of owning slaves as a justifiable result of the fall, or even as a chastisement, these sentiments were contrary to the equality of all mankind stressed in the New Testament. While initially her influence over culture was limited, the Church was later able to stand firmly in opposition to the atrocity of slavery. In 1453, Pope Eugene IV heard of Portuguese slave traders in the Canary Islands and issued a fierce order to release all men and women at once. With the discovery of the New World, slavery became more of an issue, leading Pope Paul III in 1537 to issue *Sublimis Deus*—the Most Sublime God—condemning all slavery in the New World. With the white slave owners slow to heed this censure, Pope Benedict XIV condemned slavery in the New World again with *Immensa Pastorum* in 1741. Pope Pius IX reviled slavery globally as well, calling it "the supreme villainy." The patron of slaves is St. Peter Claver, who spent a lifetime ministering to the Africans in the filthy hulls of the slave ships traveling to South America.

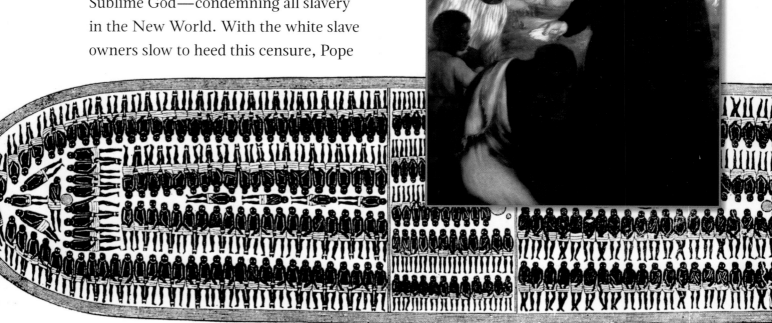

(*above*) Drawing showing how of people were packed in a slave ship, 1842 / Photo © Tallandier / Bridgeman Images. A Jesuit Missionary, perhaps Manuel de Nobrega or Peter Claver, Baptizing Blacks (oil on canvas), Spanish School, (18th century) / Private Collection / Photo © Christie's Images / Bridgeman Images

(*above*) Francois de Paris (engraving) (b/w photo), French School, (18th century) / Musee d'Art et d'Histoire, Argenteuil, France / Bridgeman Images

Jansenists crafted a new crucifix to symbolically meet their theology that Christ only died for a select few 72

In 1713, Pope Clement XI issued an apostolic constitution condemning a Catholic form of Calvinism known as Jansenism. Cornelius Jansen, bishop of Ypres, established his own rigorism that lamented the radical toxicity of original sin and the utter immorality of humanity. He taught that God gives his grace only to the predestined and that the saved are few in number. In fact, the Jansenists even crafted crucifixes with Christ's arms not at ninety degrees, universally embracing all, but suspended from the crossbeam to signify how Jesus died only for a select few. Against such pessimism, Pope Clement reemphasized God's universal love for all, affirmed the inherent goodness of the human person, and condemned the Jansenist belief that Holy Communion should not be frequently received.

(*above*) Signing the Declaration of Independence, 4th July 1776, c.1817 (oil on canvas), Trumbull, John (1756-1843) / US Capitol Collection, Washington D.C., USA / Photo © Boltin Picture Library / Bridgeman Images

73 Charles Carroll was the only Catholic to sign the Declaration of Independence

Puritans seeking religious freedom set sail on the Mayflower and were the first of many Christian denominations to settle in America. According to early American Protestant missionaries like Cotton Mather, Christians left England in order to fully embrace their beliefs. New England thus became an eclectic mix of Anglican and other Reformed influences.

Meanwhile, the Catholic Church got a slow start. By 1775, Catholics made up less than one percent of the population in the thirteen colonies. In fact, Charles Carroll was the only Catholic to sign the Declaration of Independence. The growth of Catholicism in the United States picked up steam thanks to waves of immigrants from Italy and Ireland.

The Church made great contributions to the world of mathematics

(*left*) Maria Gaetana Agnesi (engraving), Italian School, (18th century) / Private Collection / Bridgeman Images. (*right*) Blaise Pascal (1623-62) from 'Gallery of Portraits', published in 1833 (engraving), English School, (19th century) / Private Collection / Ken Welsh / Bridgeman Images.

Maria Agnesi was one of the most brilliant mathematicians of the Early Modern Period. By the time she was twenty, her *Analytical Institutions* had become a groundbreaking work in differential and integral calculus. In 1750, despite the patriarchal strictures of the Italian university system, Pope Benedict XIV intervened and personally installed Agnesi as the Chair of Mathematics and Natural Philosophy at the University of Bologna. As stellar as Maria's con-tributions to mathematics and physics were, she was not alone. One of the great Catholic philosophers and polymaths, Blaise Pascal, not only wrote theological aphorisms, but gave us Pascal's Triangle, laid the foundations for mathematical probability, and even invented the syringe and the roulette wheel. The priest and spiritual writer Francesco Faà Bruno developed the formula for identifying higher derivatives and was beatified by St. John Paul II in 1988.

(*above*) The Founding of the City of St. Augustine, Florida (colour litho), Meltzoff, Stanley (1917-2006) / National Geographic Creative / Silverfish Press/ National Geographic Creative / Bridgeman Images

75 Many towns and cities across America have Catholic names

When Pedro Aviles landed in Florida on August 28, 1565—the feast day of Augustine of Hippo—he dutifully named this city St. Augustine, foreshadowing how Catholic missionaries would name other places throughout the United States. The Spanish and French in particular spread the gospel quickly, evidenced by the preponderance of cities named after Catholic figures. Fathers Marquette and Charlevoix have lent their names to towns in the Midwest, while the West and South are peppered with similar acknowledgments—Corpus Christi, St. Mary, San Francisco, Los Angeles, San Bernardino, and Maryland—to name just a few.

Napoleon held the pope hostage

From 1789–1799, the French Revolution threatened much of what European Christians held dear. Anticlericalism was rampant and the French government imposed their radical democratization on the more traditional aspects of Christianity, seeking to control ecclesial affairs, seizing much of the Church's coffers, and insisting that clerics profess an oath of compliance. When Pope Pius VI spoke out against these injustices, Napoleon marched into Italy and took the aged pope hostage. He dragged Pius back to Valence where the Holy Father perished abject and alone, while Napoleon crowned himself emperor of the French in Notre Dame Cathedral in 1804.

(*below*) Meeting between Napoleon I (1769-1821) and Pope Pius VII (1742-1823) in the Forest of Fontainebleau in 1804, 1808 (oil on canvas), Dunouy, Alexandre Hyacinthe (1757-1841) / Chateau de Fontainebleau, Seine-et-Marne, France / Bridgeman Images

77 The Enlightenment challenged the reality of miracles and other aspects of the faith

The Age of the Enlightenment insisted on pure reason (rationalism) to know truths which were observable, quantifiable, and repeatable. Enlightenment thinkers challenged Christianity's need for faith and the idea of morality as a heavenly reward, redefining it as a way of improving this world only. One important by-product of such thinking was Deism, the likening of God to a supreme clockmaker who brought the created order into being and then left it to its own physical and mechanical laws. As such, miracles came under great suspicion in the Enlightenment, the need for personal prayer was slowly dismissed, and most theological thought was relegated to personal opinions and emotions.

(*above*) Jean-Baptiste Colbert (1619-83) Presenting the Members of the Royal Academy of Science to Louis XIV (1638-1715) c.1667 (oil on canvas) (detail) (see also 104626), Testelin, Henri (1616-95) / Château de Versailles, France / Bridgeman Images

John Keble and John Henry Newman ignited the Oxford Movement in the nineteenth century

78

Catholicism was emancipated by the British Parliament in 1829, granting "papists" basic civil rights, freedom from inordinate taxation, and other centuries-long restrictions. In 1833, Oxford dons John Keble and John Henry Newman ignited the Oxford Movement, calling for an Anglican return to Eucharistic worship, religious orders, and other reforms, thus bringing accusations of "Romanizing" against them. Keble and Newman, among others, became known as Tractarians due to their illuminating tracts advancing Anglicanism as a "third branch" (along with Catholicism and Orthodoxy) of Christ's original Church. Ultimately unsatisfied with this arrangement, Newman entered the Roman Catholic Church in 1845, established the Birmingham Oratory, and was made a cardinal in 1879 in recognition for his theological contributions to English-speaking Christianity and his defense of the Catholic faith.

(*above*) The apparition of the Blessed Virgin Mary surrounded by stars in the grotto of Lourdes. Photo © GoneWithTheWind / Shutterstock.

79 Mary was given the title the Immaculate Conception in 1854

From very early on, theologians have pondered whether Mary was conceived without original sin. This debate was finally settled in 1854 when Pope Pius IX made the first infallible statement regarding Mary's Immaculate Conception, declaring that by the grace of God, and in virtue of the merits of Jesus Christ, Mary was preserved from original sin. Not long after this, Mary appeared at Lourdes to the young Bernadette Soubirous. Interestingly, Bernadette had no knowledge of what Pius had decreed, and yet she claimed that the vision had called herself the Immaculate Conception.

The First Vatican Council was the first ecumenical council to be held at St. Peter's Basilica

Pope Pius IX's pontificate spanned more than three decades (1846–1878), the longest pontificate to date. This was a tumultuous time in Europe especially. In 1859, Charles Darwin published his *On the Origin of Species*, and in 1867 Karl Marx released *Das Kapital*. In response to these and other contemporary pieces, Pius IX issued his *Syllabus of Errors*, condemn-

ing what he judged to be a dangerous rationalism and creeping atheism. In 1867, he called for the First Vatican Council, so named because this was the first ecumenical council to be held in St. Peter's Basilica. The purpose of Vatican I was to address the various intellectual and political challenges of the age.

(*above*) The opening of the First Vatican Council on 8th December 1869, c.1870 (colour litho), French School, (19th century) / Bibliotheque Nationale, Paris, France / Archives Charmet / Bridgeman Images

81 The Catholic Church is the oldest functioning legal system

From the Theodosian Code of the mid-fifth century to Gratian's collection of laws known as the *Decretum* in 1140, and up through modern forms of Canon Law, one of the Church's greatest contributions to the world has been to uphold the natural rights of all. The Church has always seen basic human rights as rooted in the inalienable dignity of every human person. The Catholic Church is thus responsible for protecting and promoting such fundamental rights like the right to life, to own private property, to marry, and to be presumed innocent until proven guilty. The Church has always stressed that these rights belong to every human person and should not depend on any government or ruler.

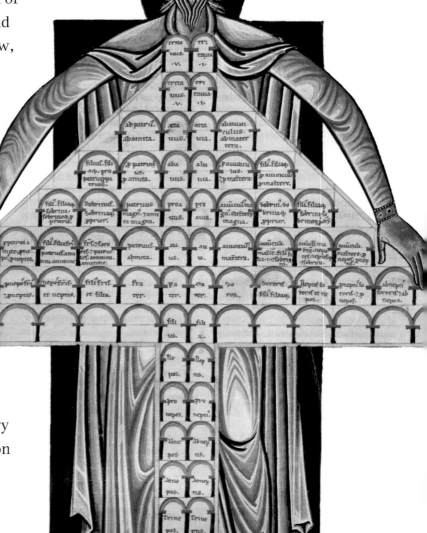

(*right*) The *Decretum Gratiani*, also known as the Concordia discordantium canonum or Concordantia discordantium canonum, is a collection of Canon law compiled and written in the 12th century as a legal textbook by the jurist known as Gratian. Consanguinity is the quality of being descended from the same ancestor as another person. The laws of many jurisdictions set out degrees of consanguinity in relation to prohibited sexual relations and marriage parties or whether a given person inherits property when a deceased person has not left a will. Ms 360 f.264v Tree of Consanguinity, from the 'Decrets de Gratien' (vellum), French School, (14th century) / Bibliotheque Municipale, Amiens, France / Bridgeman Images.

(*left*) Nursery & Kindergarten run by catholic nuns. Franciscan sister holding an orphan (photo) / Godong/UIG / Bridgeman Images. (*above*) Mass procession in Keur Moussa benedictine abbey (photo) / Godong/UIG / Bridgeman Images

Africa has given the Church many examples of holiness

82

Throughout history, Africa has given the Church many examples of holiness. At least three popes hale from Africa (St. Victor I, St. Miltiades, and St. Gelasius), while St. Moses the Black, martyred in Egypt around 405, was one of the early Church's most influential monks. St. Charles Lwanga and his companions were martyred for their faith on June 3, 1886 by the Ugandan king who wrongly saw Christianity as a threatening result of colonialization, and Sr. Josephine Bakhita was a Sudanese slave who gained her freedom and became a Canossian sister in Italy. She was canonized as a saint in 2000.

(*above*) His Holiness Pope Leo XIII, 1893 Engraving / Private Collection / Photo © Liszt Collection / Bridgeman Images

83 Pope Leo XIII wrote many important encyclicals

Pope Leo XIII proved to be a brilliant administrator and effective teacher, providing the Church with some of the most groundbreaking encyclicals to date. *Aeterni Patris* reinvigorated Thomas Aquinas's school of thought, sparking the Neo-Thomistic revival of the twentieth century. *Humanum Genus* condemned Freemasonry and warned against the dangers of Marxism, while *Providentissimus Deus* reinvigorated scripture studies and upheld the entire canon as divinely inspired. But it was his encyclical *Rerum Novarum* that revolutionized how Catholics began to address the social ills of the time. *Rerum Novarum* ("The Spirit of Revolutionary Change") dealt with the plight of workers brought about by the Industrial Revolution and reaffirmed the natural right to own property, among other things. At its core, it rejected many of the key tenets of Socialism.

Friedrich Nietzsche argued Christianity taught a wicked "reversal of morals"

84

One of the most influential modern critics of the Christian Church was the German philosopher Friedrich Nietzsche. Nietzsche's main thesis stated that Christianity was a wicked destroyer of human greatness masquerading as a loving and liberating faith. He believed that only the "Superman" (the Übermensch) was strong enough to live without the comforts provided by a God. He argued that we must, therefore, render God dead if the human spirit is ever going to slough off the shackles of uniformity and meekness in order to truly soar. Nietzsche argued that when Christians were unable to meet the Romans on their own terms, they reversed the concept of human excellence. The Crucified Christ replaced domination with humility, and consequently made the most powerful weapon the willingness to lay down one's life. Nietzsche died lamenting how this "reversal of morals" had woefully enervated humanity from its instinct to excel and outrival all others.

(*above*) German philosopher Friedrich Wilhelm Nietzsche (1844-1900) / Bridgeman Images (right) Crucifix / photo © guillermo_bsas / Shutterstock

85 The Church continually spoke out against socio-economic injustices in the twentieth century

As socio-economic conditions continued to be a major issue in the twentieth century, the Church gave a voice and provided care to the forgotten classes of society. In 1931, Pope Pius XI issued *Quadragesimo Anno* ("In the Fortieth Year"), calling for greater solidarity among the working classes, while in 1991, St. John Paul II released *Centesimus Annus* ("The One Hundredth Year") which further advanced the Church's teaching on the dangers of communism, socialism, and unbridled capitalism. Further, Dorothy Day and Peter Maurin founded the Catholic Worker Movement in 1933 to tend to the poor who were often dismissed in bustling cities. The largest charitable organization in the United States continues to be the Catholic Church, providing millions of dollars of care for Christ's forgotten brothers and sisters.

(*above*) Dorothy Day speaks with Veronica Kane, one of the residents at House of Hospitality. (Photo by ken Korotkin/NY Daily News via Getty Images)

St. Thérèse was named a Doctor of the Church despite very little formal education

86

Carmelite spirituality reached a crescendo in the beautiful life of St. Thérèse of Lisieux, the Little Flower of Jesus. This young French girl gave the Church a new spirituality through her "little way." For that, St. Thérèse has been named a Doctor of the Church despite holding no higher academic degrees and writing only a memoire, along with some letters and poems. She is also patroness of the missions, even though she rarely left her cloistered Carmel in Normandy before succumbing to tuberculosis at the age of twenty-four. The global popularity of this little and modest child of Christ proves the validity of His words: "whoever humbles himself will be exalted" (Mt 23:12).

"What matters in life is not great deeds, but great love. . . . My mission—to make God loved—will begin after my death. I will spend my heaven doing good on earth. I will let fall a shower of roses."

—ST. THÉRÈSE OF LISIEUX, *STORY OF A SOUL*

(*above*) Left to right, Bishop William Skylstad, V.P. of the USCCB, Bishop Wilton Gregory, President of the USCCB, Msgr. William Fay, General Secr. of the USCCB, and Mr. Robert Henry, Parlimentarian, sing during the opening session of the United States Conference of Catholic Bishops at the Fairmont Hotel. (Photo by Evan Richman/The Boston Globe via Getty Images)

87

The origins of the USCCB date back to World War I

In the aftermath of World War I, the American bishops met in 1917 for the first time since 1884. They gathered over several concerns, including the traumatized state of young men returning from war, threats by the US government to have more control over Catholic education, and even the first rumblings of Prohibition. Thus, the National Catholic Welfare Council was founded in 1919 at the Catholic University of America in response to Pope Benedict XV's call for greater social justice and interaction. After Vatican II, this body split into the National Conference of Catholic Bishops (NCCB), which addressed Christian concerns affected by government policies, and the United States Catholic Conference (USCC), which looked after Church affairs. In 2001 these two bodies reunited as the United States Conference of Catholic Bishops (USCCB), the organization that exists today.

The Vatican became its own country with the Lateran Treaty of 1929

At two-tenths of a square mile and with a population of fewer than nine hundred citizens, the smallest country in the world is Vatican City. In an attempt to unify all independent lands, the Kingdom of Italy absorbed the Vatican in 1870, but the Lateran Treaty of 1929 returned autonomy to the Vatican, thereby liberating it as a separate entity from Italy's Fascist government. Today the Holy See enjoys formal diplomatic ties with 174 nations, has its own banking and postal system, and welcomes approximately five million pilgrim tourists per year.

(*below*) St. Peter's Cathedral view from the top. Photo © Sky Sajjaphot / Shutterstock

Several Catholic clergymen hypothesized about an expanding universe before Einstein

The Church has always been a pioneer in the area of astronomical sciences. The world's most advanced telescopic lenses are found at the Specola Vaticana, the observatories in Italy and in Arizona, both run by the Vatican. The bishop of Lincoln, Robert Grosseteste, advanced an early version of the "Big Bang" theory of the cosmos. He theorized that the rest of creation was the unfolding expansion of this initial explosion of light. But it was really the Belgian priest George Lemaître who first proposed this theory of the universe's expansion. In 1927, two years before Edwin Hubble's famous essay on the subject, and years before Einstein's groundbreaking hypotheses, Father Lemaître wrote up his theory of what he called this "primeval atom," stating that the cosmos originated from an initial burst of light and has grown outward in a constant state of expansion ever since.

(*above*) Albert Einstein (1879-1955) and Georges Lemaitre abbot, inventor of Big Bang theory in 1933 / Bridgeman Images

(*above*) Mathematician and friend of Leonardo da Vinci; Pacioli consults a printed edition of Euclid's Elements which he illustrates by drawing an equilateral triangle inside a circle. Portrait of Luca Pacioli (c.1445-c.1514) 1495 (oil on panel), Barbari, Jacopo de' (1440/50-a.1515) / Museo e Gallerie Nazionale di Capodimonte, Naples, Italy / Bridgeman Images

A Franciscan monk invented the method of double-entry bookkeeping

90

Luca Bartolomeo de Pacioli, a fifteenth-century Franciscan, was a friend of Leonardo da Vinci and a well-known polymath and inventor in his own right. Brother Luca wrote books on chess and encyclopedias of math, but his greatest contribution was organizing debits and credits into two columns for businesses—a method known as double-entry bookkeeping. This system allowed merchants to see how their equity should always be equal to their assets, minus their liabilities. Many historians see this development as the basis for modern day capitalism.

(*above*) Roberto Busa at the control console of the IBM 705, IBM World Headquarters, 590 Madison Avenue, New York, 1958. [IBM Archives]. The image shown here is kindly made available under a Creative Commons CC-BY-NC license by permission of CIRCSE Research Centre, Università Cattolica del Sacro Cuore, Milan, Italy. The original document pictured in the image is contained in the "Busa Archive," held in the library of the same university. For further information, or to request permission for reuse, please contact Marco Passarotti, on marco.passarotti AT unicatt.it, or by post: Largo Gemelli 1, 20123 Milan, Italy.

91 A Jesuit priest created the first hypertext

The first electronic text with hyper-links was the *Summa Theologiae* by St. Thomas Aquinas. In 1949, Father Roberto Busa, an Italian Jesuit priest, met with the founder of IBM to sponsor the compilation of the works of Aquinas. The project lasted thirty years and eventually produced fifty-six printed volumes of the Index Thomisticus. During his work, Busa discovered a way of embedding a link into a word on the screen and connecting the reader to related information by simply clicking on that highlighted term, a connection Busa called a hyper-text. The Alliance of Digital Humanities Organizations, a group dedicated to foster-ing greater collaboration between technol-ogy and the humanities, awards an annual "Busa Prize," honoring achievements in this new field of "humanities computing."

Pope Pius XII fought against the evils of Nazism

The future Pope Pius XII, Eugenio Pacelli, began his Vatican work as the nuncio to Germany during a particularly tragic period under the Nazi regime. As nuncio, he insisted that Pope Pius XI's 1937 encyclical *Mit Brennender Sorge* (With Burning Anxiety) be smuggled into Germany and proclaimed from every pulpit. When that tactic backfired, costing many Catholic and Jewish lives, Pope Pius XII decided to work more covertly, secretly housing and smuggling Jewish families to safety. Shortly after his death, attempts were made to depict the pontiff as a Nazi sympathizer. Today, more supportive works are emerging that detail the pope's efforts *against* Nazi Germany.

(*above*) Pope Pius XII (b/w photo) / © SZ Photo / Bridgeman Images

93 "Good Pope John" was so popular that he was canonized after only one confirmed miracle

Angelo Giussepe Roncalli reclaimed the name of an anti-pope, John XXIII, a fitting opening to his papacy, which sought reconciliation across the globe and the centuries. Pope John convened the Second Vatican Council, played a pivotal role in the peaceful conclusion of the Cuban Missile Crisis, and was the first pope to ever grace the cover of TIME, being "Man of the Year" in 1962.

He was also the first pope in over two hundred years to attend the theater, and broke many papal precedents by visiting prisons and hospitals unescorted and unannounced. He was canonized a saint alongside John Paul II with only one miracle instead of the normal two, attesting to his wide popularity and the people's admiration of the "Good Pope John."

94 The Second Vatican Council was called to address the needs of Christians in the twentieth century

In 1959, St. John XXIII convened the Second Vatican Council to update the application of the gospel in the contemporary world. More than 2,600 bishops and expert theologians gathered to discuss the nature of the Church and address the new needs of Christians that had arisen during the twentieth century. Vernacular languages were promoted and the liturgy revised, religious life was encouraged to eliminate medieval accretions and reclaim its original charisma, and sixteen illuminating documents were produced that are still being discussed and understood today.

(*opposite*) Second Vatican Council Convened in 1963 (photo) / St. Peter's, Vatican City / Bridgeman Images

95 *Humanae Vitae* accurately prophesized the moral decay of the twentieth century

Even though he would reign for another ten years, Pope Paul VI issued his last encyclical in 1968. Reportedly defeated by the lukewarm reception his teaching received from his priests, Paul VI's *Humanae Vitae* revealed a noticeable split in the Church that had been unseen for centuries. Upholding the fecundity of marriage against the onslaught of modern contraceptives becoming mainstream, Paul VI propheti-cally declared that if a contraceptive men-tality ever took hold of a culture, society at all levels would suffer a general lowering of morality, adultery and marital infidelity would increase, men would eventually lose the due reverence owed to women, and governmentally mandated contraceptive and family-sized policies would infringe upon the inherent rights of the family.

(*below*) Pope Paul VI (Giovanni Battista Montini), during Eucharistic congress in Pisa June 13, 1965 / Bridgeman Images.

(*above*) Funeral Procession for Pope John Paul I (Albino Luciani) 1978 (b/w photo), Italian Photographer, (20th century) / Alinari / Bridgeman Images

John Paul I was pope for just thirty-three days

96

The last time the Church saw three popes in one year was 1605 (Clement VIII, Leo XI, and Paul V). In the late summer of 1978, however, Pope Paul VI died and Albino Luciani, Patriarch of Venice, was elected pope. He took the name John Paul I, the first pontiff ever to take a double name, honoring his predecessors John XXIII and Paul VI. His reign lasted from August 26 to September 28, only thirty-three days. He was found dead lying in his bed with an open book beside him. It was later determined he probably died of a heart attack, but his sudden death gave rise to all sorts of fanciful conspiracy theories. Even with such a short reign, Pope John Paul I captured the affection of the world and was beloved by all.

1983 - Portrait of Pope John Paul II. / Forum / Bridgeman Images

A Polish playwright became the first-ever Slavic pope

On October 16, 1978 the Church elected her first Slavic pope and the first non-Italian pope in over four hundred years. As a young man in Poland, Karol Wojtła was drawn to the arts, appearing in stage productions and writing plays and poetry. A staunch opponent of the Nazis and later the Communists, Wojtła preached and wrote on the inalienable God-given dignity of the human person and the beauty of the traditional family as a way of defeating all oppressive regimes. As an auxiliary bishop of Kraków, he proved very influential at Vatican II and was elected to the papacy on October 16, 1978. John Paul was canonized in 2014 by Pope Francis.

John Paul II's writings had a profound impact on Church History

Saint John Paul II's twenty-seven-year papacy is the second longest to date after Pius IX, and under his guidance the Church issued some of her most important documents. In 1983, St. John Paul reworked the old 1917 Code of Canon Law, incorporating more Vatican II theology. In 1992, he released the *Catechism of the Catholic Church*, the first official catechism since the Council of Trent's *Roman Catechism*. John Paul also wrote fourteen papal encyclicals on a wide range of important topics, beginning with *Redemptoris Hominis* (The Redeemer of Humankind) in 1979 that set the tone of his papacy, placing Jesus Christ as the sole and supreme guarantor of human worth and dignity. He also wrote such groundbreaking ethical works like *Veritatis Splendor* (On the Beauty of Truth) and *Evangelium Vitae* (On the Gospel of Life) that had profound implications on Church teaching in the modern world.

99 Pope Benedict XVI became the first pope to step down in over 700 years

There is no requirement that a pope has to die in office. In 2013, to the surprise of the world, Pope Benedict XVI became the first pope to retire since Pope Celestine V in 1294. After serving the Church as the Head of the Congregation of the Doctrine of the Faith from 1981–2005, Joseph Ratzinger was elected to succeed his dear friend, John Paul II. An introverted scholar and former arch-bishop of Munich and Freising, Ratzinger took the name Benedict to highlight the Church's need to return to prayer and work. Major themes of his pontificate included restoring the sacredness of the liturgy, renewing the serious study of the-ology, and placing Vatican II into a more secure "hermeneutic of continuity," argu-ing that the abuses and the excesses seen in the Church immediately afterwards were unintended aber-rations and not to be considered the norm.

(*right*) Pope Benedict XVI, Vatican City, Vatican City State, 2012 (photo) / Mondadori Portfolio/Archivio Grzegorz Galazka/ Bridgeman Images

Jorge Bergoglio became a pope of many "firsts" 100

Argentinean-born Jorge Mario Bergoglio was elected pope in 2013, making him the 266th Roman Pontiff. He was the first Jesuit, the first American, the first from the southern hemisphere, and the first pope to have taken the name Francis. His warmth and relative sim-plicity endeared him to many, especially those who have grown cynical regarding Christianity and the Church in the twenty-first century. His two encyclicals, *Lumen Fidei* and *Laudato Si'*, were the first-ever papal encyclicals dealing with the Christian care for the environment.

(*above*) The Second Coming, 1794 (egg tempera & gold leaf on panel), Abraham (18th century) / Benaki Museum, Athens, Greece / Gift of A. Kalenderi in memory of A. and E. Kinatzoglou / Bridgeman Images

101

The Church has never speculated about when the Second Coming will occur

Regardless of what happens hereafter, the final entry in any Church history list must reference the last day. If it weren't for Jerome, we wouldn't have the term "rapture." It comes from the Latin of 1 Thessalonians 4:17—"then we who are alive, who are left, shall be caught up [rapiemur] together with them in the clouds to meet the Lord in the air." While there is much speculation about how this rapture will occur, the Catholic Church has never proposed dates for when this will happen or how it will occur. We believe that there will be days of final trial that will reveal the fullness of iniquity, and that through this "final Passover" the Son of God will appear again and his definitive victory "will take the form of the Last Judgment after the final cosmic upheaval of this passing world" (CCC 677).

About the author

Father David Meconi, S.J., holds a Doctorate in Philosophy from Oxford University, England and the Pontifical Licentiate in Greek and Latin Patristic Theology from University of Innsbruck, Austria. He currently teaches as Assistant Professor of Patristic Studies at Saint Louis University. His books include *Catherine Doherty: Essential Writings* (Orbis Press, 2009), *Frank Sheed and Maisie Ward: Spiritual Writings* (Orbis Press, 2010), and *The One Christ: St. Augustine's Theology of Deification* (Catholic University of America Press). He is also a Catholic Course instructor for *The First 500 Years: The Fathers, Councils, and Doctrines of the Early Church*. Fr. Meconi is the editor of *Homiletic and Pastoral Review*, and his articles have appeared in the *Journal of Ecclesiastical History*, *Augustinian Studies*, *International Philosophical Quarterly*, and *New Oxford Review*.

Saint Benedict Press

Saint Benedict Press publishes books, Bibles, and multimedia that explore and defend the Catholic intellectual tradition. Our mission is to present the truths of the Catholic faith in an attractive and accessible manner.

Founded in 2006, our name pays homage to the guiding influence of the Rule of Saint Benedict and the Benedictine monks of Belmont Abbey, just a short distance from our headquarters in Charlotte, NC.

Saint Benedict Press publishes under several imprints. Our TAN Books imprint (TANBooks.com), publishes over 500 titles in theology, spirituality, devotions, Church doctrine, history, and the Lives of the Saints. Our Catholic Courses imprint (CatholicCourses.com) publishes audio and video lectures from the world's best professors in Theology, Philosophy, Scripture, Literature and more.

For a free catalog, visit us online at
TANBooks.com

Or call us toll-free at
(800) 437-5876